A Pyramid Cookery Paperback

Cocktails

Notes for American readers

The measure that has been used in the recipes is based on a bar jigger, which is 25 ml (1 fl oz). If preferred, a different volume can be used providing the proportions are kept constant within a drink and suitable adjustments are made to spoon measurements, where they occur.

Standard level spoon measurements are used in all recipes.
1 tablespoon = one 15 ml spoon
1 teaspoon = one 5 ml spoon
Imperial and metric measurements have been given in some of the recipes. Use one set of measurements only and not a mixture of both.

UK	US
caster sugar	granulated sugar
cocktail cherries	maraschino cherries
cocktail stick	toothpick
double cream	heavy cream
drinking chocolate	presweetened cocoa powder
icing sugar	confectioners' sugar
jug	pitcher
lemon rind	lemon peel or zest
single cream	light cream
soda water	club soda

SAFETY NOTE

The Department of Health advises that eggs should not be consumed raw. This book contains recipes made with raw eggs. It is prudent for more vulnerable people such as pregnant and nursing mothers, invalids and the elderly to avoid these recipes.

An Hachette Livre UK Company

www.hachettelivre.co.uk

A Pyramid Paperback

First published in Great Britain in 2002 by

Hamlyn, a division of Octopus Publishing Group Ltd

2–4 Heron Quays, London E14 4JP

ISBN 978-0-600-61765-5

A CIP catalogue record for this book is available from the British Library

Printed and bound in China

2 4 6 8 10 9 7 5 3 1

Contents

Cocktails

Cocktails are iced alcoholic drinks with a subtle and harmonious blend of flavours and a powerful kick; spirits are at the heart of most true cocktails. They are surprisingly easy to make, provided you remember a couple of simple rules. Keep all your ingredients in a cool place, and serve chilled drinks in chilled glasses. Wash mixing equipment between making different cocktails to avoid mixing flavours, and rinse spoons and other stirrers.

Equipment

The three basic pieces of cocktail equipment are a shaker, a blender and a mixing glass. Drinks with ingredients such as egg whites, syrups and fruit are shaken, then strained to remove any items like bits of ice and fruit that could spoil the look of the drink. A blender is useful for drinks that contain fresh fruit, ice cream and milk and require a more thorough shaking. It is also useful for smoothies and similar drinks. The mixing glass is used for drinks that require only a gentle stirring before they are poured, or strained, into glasses. Other essential equipment are a chopping board and a sharp knife, ice trays for freezing ice and tongs to lift it, a corkscrew, a lemon squeezer and a supply of tea towels. A set of bar measures, an ice bucket and glass swizzle sticks are nice to have around but not absolutely vital.

Ice

This is one of the most important ingredients when mixing drinks and you should never skimp on it – it really does make all the difference. If you are having a party, make the ice in advance and store it in the freezer. Tip the ice cubes into a polythene bag and squirt them with soda water – this will stop them from sticking to each other. Some cocktails need cracked ice. To make this, put the ice cubes in a polythene bag and hit hard with a rolling pin. To make crushed ice, which cools a drink more effectively, and faster than cracked ice, simply continuing hammering until the ice is in smaller pieces. The more ice you use, the cooler a drink will be, but remember that too much ice will also dilute a drink. This is particularly true of crushed ice.

Sugar Syrup

This is the most practical way of sweetening a drink. Since the sugar is already dissolved it does not need lengthy stirring to blend it into a cold drink. To make sugar syrup, pour equal quantities of sugar and water (6 tablespoons of each is a sensible amount) into a small saucepan and bring to the boil, stirring to dissolve the sugar, then boil for 1–2 minutes without stirring. Sugar syrup can be stored in the refrigerator in a sterilized bottle for up to 2 months.

Salty Dog (see page 54)

Vodka Sea Breeze (see page 80)

Zombie (see page 14)

Rum Cocktails

DAIQUIRIS AND ZOMBIES

DAIQUIRI 10

BANANA DAIQUIRI 10

APRICOT DAIQUIRI 10

COCONUT DAIQUIRI 10

STRAWBERRY DAIQUIRI 12

FROZEN PINEAPPLE DAIQUIRI 12

MELON DAIQUIRI 12

ZOMBIE 14

HAVANA ZOMBIE 14

ZOMBIE CHRISTOPHE 14

ZOMBIE PRINCE 14

EXOTIC COCKTAILS

GRENADA 16

PINA COLADA 16

BLUE HAWAIIAN 16

MAI TAI 18

SUMMERTIME 18

BANANA ROYAL 18

PORT ANTONIO 18

DISCOVERY BAY 20

ST LUCIA 20

BAHAMAS 20

SERENADE 20

PUSSYFOOT 22

VIRGIN'S PRAYER 22

BOMBAY SMASH 22

TROPICAL DREAM 22

PUNCHES AND FIZZES

FLORIDA SKIES 24

CUBA LIBRE 24

MISSISSIPPI PUNCH 24

HAVANA BEACH 24

TOBAGO FIZZ 26

NEW ORLEANS DANDY 26

BAHAMAS PUNCH 26

PINK RUM 26

GOLDEN RUM PUNCH 28

PINK TREASURE 28

PUNCH JULIEN 28

SLOW SIPPERS

ALEXANDER BABY 30

RUM MARTINI 30

BATISTE 30

HONEYSUCKLE 30

BLACK WIDOW 30

WHITE WITCH 32

SUNSET TEA 32

HEARTWARMER 32

BETWEEN THE SHEETS 32

ISLAND CREAM GROG 32

Rum

Rum has a strange mixture of associations, from smugglers risking shipwreck and capture, to the free tipple that kept the British Navy happy, and to wealthy planters relaxing on sunny verandahs, sipping long fruit-decked concoctions.

'Hot, Hellish and Terrible'

Christopher Columbus is said to have introduced sugar cane to the Caribbean. While this may be mere legend, it is undoubtedly true that rum, the spirit distilled from it, reached the rest of the world from the Caribbean. By the seventeenth century distillation from sugar cane or its products was taking place in Hispaniola, to produce a spirit that a contemporary described as 'hot, hellish and terrible'. Over the years, rum became more palatable as new techniques were discovered. From being a rough spirit that only colonists drank for want of anything better, rum became a popular drink, first in western Europe and later throughout the world. The right of British sailors to a daily rum ration was enshrined in the Royal Navy and was not abolished until 1970.

Island Variations

Rum is distilled from molasses and, in some cases, directly from the fermented juices of the sugar cane. To begin with, it is a colourless, high-strength spirit with little natural flavour. Caramel may then be added to give colour, and some premium rums also acquire colour while maturing in oak casks.

Basically, there are three types of rum – white, golden or light, and dark. Various flavourings are also added and it is common for rums from different places to be blended. Rum is produced wherever sugar cane grows but, arguably, the Caribbean produces the best and each island group has its own type. Martinique and Jamaica are well known for pungent, sweet, heavy-bodied dark rums. Paler, drier and lighter golden rums are widely produced, especially in Cuba, Puerto Rico and Barbados. Puerto Rico is also the largest producer of white rum, but this is made in many other places, too.

Rum as a Cocktail Base

White rum is a popular base for cocktails, as it blends easily with a wide range of flavours. Many classics – Daiquiri, Piña Colada, Blue Hawaiian and Mai Tai – are white rum cocktails. Darker rums combine superbly with fruit juices, especially lime, and are perfect for cold or hot punches. Some cocktails, such as the Zombie, are based on a mixture of different types of rum and, perhaps surprisingly, although it has a strong flavour itself, rum combines well with other spirits and liqueurs.

Sunset Tea (see page 32)

Daiquiris and Zombies

Wonderfully refreshing, these are classic cocktails, where rum is partnered with fruit – freshly squeezed or in the form of a fruit liqueur.

Daiquiri

Serves 1
cracked ice
juice of 2 limes
1 teaspoon sugar syrup (see page 4)
3 measures white rum

Put lots of cracked ice in a cocktail shaker. Pour the lime juice, sugar syrup and rum over the ice. Shake thoroughly until a frost forms, then strain into a chilled cocktail glass.

Banana Daiquiri

Serves 1
3 cracked ice cubes
2 measures white rum
½ measure banana liqueur
½ small banana
½ measure lime cordial
to decorate
1 teaspoon powdered sugar (optional)
banana slice

Put the cracked ice in a margarita glass or tall goblet. Put the rum, banana liqueur, banana and lime cordial in a blender and blend for 30 seconds. Pour into the glass and decorate with the powdered sugar, if using, and banana slice.

Apricot Daiquiri

Serves 1
crushed ice
1 measure white rum
1 measure lemon juice
½ measure apricot liqueur or brandy
3 ripe apricots, peeled and pitted
to decorate
apricot slice
cocktail cherry
mint sprig

Put some crushed ice in a blender. Add the rum, lemon juice, apricot liqueur or brandy and the apricots and blend for 1 minute, or until the mixture is smooth. Pour into a chilled cocktail glass and decorate with an apricot slice, a cocktail cherry and a mint sprig.

Coconut Daiquiri

Serves 1
crushed ice
2 measures coconut liqueur
2 measures fresh lime juice
1 measure white rum
1 dash egg white
lime slice, to decorate

Put the ice in a cocktail shaker and add all the ingredients. Shake vigorously until a frost forms. Strain and pour into a chilled cocktail glass. Decorate with a slice of lime.

Daiquiri

Banana Daiquiri

Happy accident

The Daiquiri was created by an American mining engineer working in Cuba in 1896. He was expecting VIP guests and his supplies of gin had run out, so he extemporized with rum – and created this classic cocktail.

Strawberry Daiquiri

Serves 1
1 measure white rum
½ measure crème de fraises
½ measure fresh lemon juice
4 ripe strawberries, hulled
crushed ice
to decorate
strawberry slice
mint sprig

Put the rum, crème de fraises, lemon juice, strawberries and ice in a food processor or blender and process at a slow speed for 5 seconds, then at high speed for about 20 seconds. Pour into a chilled glass and decorate with a strawberry slice and a mint sprig.

Variation

This fruity cocktail is especially delicious if you make it with crème de fraises des bois, a wild strawberry liqueur.

Frozen Pineapple Daiquiri

Serves 1
crushed ice
2–3 pineapple slices
½ measure fresh lime juice
1 measure white rum
¼ measure Cointreau
1 teaspoon sugar syrup (see page 4)
piece of pineapple, to decorate

Put some crushed ice in a blender and add the pineapple slices, lime juice, white rum, Cointreau and sugar syrup. Blend at the highest speed until smooth, then pour into a chilled cocktail glass. Decorate with a piece of fresh pineapple and serve with a straw.

Melon Daiquiri

Serves 1
2 measures white rum
1 measure fresh lime juice
2 dashes Midori
2 scoops crushed ice

Put the white rum, lime juice and liqueur in a blender with the crushed ice and blend until smooth. Serve in a chilled goblet with straws.

Strawberry Daiquiri

Did you know?
Midori is a Japanese melon liqueur. Combined with rum and lime juice, it makes a delectable drink.

Zombie
Serves I
3 cracked ice cubes
I measure dark rum
I measure white rum
½ measure golden rum
½ measure apricot brandy
juice of ½ lime
2 measures unsweetened pineapple juice
2 teaspoons powdered sugar
to decorate
kiwi fruit slice
cocktail cherry
pineapple wedge
powdered sugar (optional)

Place a tall glass in the freezer so the outside becomes frosted. Put the ice in a cocktail shaker. Add the rums, apricot brandy, lime juice, pineapple juice and sugar. Shake to mix. Pour into the glass without straining. To decorate, spear the slice of kiwi fruit, cherry and pineapple with a cocktail stick and place it across the top of the glass, balanced on the rim. Sprinkle the powdered sugar over the top and serve.

Did you know?
Zombies contain all three types of rum – dark, golden and white. The darker rums are aged in charred oak casks while white rums are aged in stainless steel tanks.

Havana Zombie
Serves I
4–5 ice cubes
juice of I lime
5 tablespoons pineapple juice
I teaspoon sugar syrup (see page 4)
I measure white rum
I measure golden rum
I measure dark rum

Put the ice cubes in a mixing glass. Pour the lime juice, pineapple juice, sugar syrup and rums over the ice and stir vigorously. Pour, without straining, into a tall glass.

Zombie Christophe
Serves I
4–5 ice cubes
juice of I lime or lemon
juice of ½ orange
250 ml (8 fl oz) unsweetened pineapple juice
I measure blue Curaçao
I measure white rum
I measure golden rum
½ measure dark rum
to decorate
lime or lemon slice
mint sprig

Put the ice cubes in a mixing glass. Pour the lime or lemon juice, orange juice, pineapple juice, Curaçao, white and golden rums over the ice. Stir vigorously, then pour, without straining, into a tumbler. Top with the dark rum, stir gently and serve decorated with a slice of lime or lemon and a mint sprig.

Zombie Prince
Serves I
crushed ice
juice of I lemon
juice of I orange
juice of ½ grapefruit
3 drops Angostura bitters
I teaspoon soft brown sugar
I measure white rum
I measure golden rum
I measure dark rum
to decorate
lime slice
orange slice

Put the crushed ice in a mixing glass. Pour the lemon, orange and grapefruit juices over the ice and splash in the bitters. Add the sugar and pour in the three rums. Stir vigorously, then pour, without straining, into a Collins glass. Decorate with slices of lime and orange.

Zombie

Zombie Christophe

Did you know?

A Collins glass is perfect for long drinks. These glasses are narrow with slightly tapered or perfectly straight sides.

Angostura bitters were developed in the Venezuelan town of Angostura in the nineteenth century as a specific against malaria. It is reputed to contain more than 40 plant extracts including cinnamon, gentian, orange peel, cloves and nutmeg, as well as bark from the angostura and cinchona trees.

Zombie Prince

Exotic Cocktails

Discover the astonishing versatility of rum. Mix it with a wide range of other ingredients – from Curaçao in a St Lucia to coconut milk in a Piña Colada.

Grenada

Serves 1
4–5 ice cubes
juice of ½ orange
1 measure sweet vermouth
3 measures golden or dark rum
ground cinnamon, to decorate

Put the ice cubes in a mixing glass. Pour the orange juice, vermouth and rum over the ice. Stir vigorously, then strain into a chilled cocktail glass. Sprinkle a little ground cinnamon on top.

Piña Colada

Serves 1
cracked ice
1 measure white rum
2 measures coconut milk (see opposite)
2 measures pineapple juice
to decorate
strawberry slice
mango slice
pineapple slice

Put some cracked ice, the rum, coconut milk and pineapple juice in a cocktail shaker. Shake lightly to mix. Strain into a large glass and decorate with the slices of strawberry, mango and pineapple.

Blue Hawaiian

Serves 1
crushed ice
1 measure white rum
½ measure blue Curaçao
2 measures pineapple juice
1 measure coconut cream (see opposite)
pineapple wedge, to decorate

Put some crushed ice in a blender and pour in the rum, blue Curaçao, pineapple juice and coconut cream. Blend at high speed for 20–30 seconds. Pour into a chilled cocktail glass and decorate with a pineapple wedge.

Grenada

Coconuts explained

Coconut water is the thin liquid found inside a fresh coconut whereas coconut milk can be made by blending fresh coconut, grated creamed coconut or desiccated coconut with hot water. Coconut water and coconut milk are sold in cans; the thicker coconut cream comes in 200 ml (7 fl oz) packs.

Blue Hawaiian

Mai Tai

Serves I

lightly beaten egg white
caster sugar, for frosting
I measure white rum
½ measure orange juice
½ measure lime juice
3 ice cubes, crushed
to decorate
cocktail cherries
pineapple cubes
orange slice

Dip the rim of a tall glass into the beaten egg white, then into the caster sugar. Put the rum, orange juice and lime juice in a cocktail shaker. Shake to mix. Put the ice in the glass and pour the cocktail over it. Decorate with the cherries, pineapple and orange slice.

Did you know?
The name of this cocktail is taken from the Tahitian and means 'good', which it certainly is.

Summertime

Serves I

3 cracked ice cubes
I ½ measures **Grand Marnier or Cointreau**
½ measure **dark rum**
2 teaspoons **lemon juice**
lemon slice, to decorate

Put the ice cubes in a cocktail shaker and add the Grand Marnier or Cointreau, rum and lemon juice. Shake well. Strain into a cocktail glass and decorate with the slice of lemon.

Banana Royal

Serves I

crushed ice
I ½ measures coconut milk (see page 17)
3 measures pineapple juice
I ½ measures golden rum
½ measure double cream
I ripe banana
grated coconut, to decorate

Put some crushed ice in a blender and add the coconut milk, pineapple juice, rum, cream and banana. Blend at high speed for 15–30 seconds, until smooth and creamy. Pour into an old-fashioned glass and sprinkle with grated coconut.

Port Antonio

Serves I

½ teaspoon grenadine
4–5 ice cubes
I measure fresh lime juice
3 measures white rum or golden rum
to decorate
lime rind
cocktail cherry

Spoon the grenadine into a chilled cocktail glass. Put the ice cubes in a mixing glass. Pour the lime juice and rum over the ice and stir vigorously, then strain into the cocktail glass. Wrap the lime rind round the cocktail cherry, spear them with a cocktail stick and use to decorate the drink.

Port Antonio

Mai Tai

Did you know?

Both Cointreau and Grand Marnier are French liqueurs flavoured with oranges. Cointreau is a colourless liquid, while Grand Marnier has a golden colour from its Cognac base.

Grenadine is a sweet non-alcoholic syrup made from pomegranates, which give it its rich rosy pink colour.

Discovery Bay

Serves I

4–5 ice cubes
3 drops Angostura bitters
juice of ½ lime
I teaspoon Curaçao or blue Curaçao
I teaspoon sugar syrup (see page 4)
3 measures golden or dark rum
lime slices, to decorate

Put the ice cubes in a cocktail shaker. Shake the bitters over the ice. Pour in the lime juice, Curaçao, sugar syrup and rum and shake until a frost forms. Strain into an old-fashioned glass. Decorate with lime slices.

St Lucia

Serves I

4–5 ice cubes
I measure Curaçao
I measure dry vermouth
juice of ½ orange
I teaspoon grenadine
2 measures white or golden rum
to decorate
orange rind spiral
cocktail cherry

Put the ice in a cocktail shaker. Pour the Curaçao, dry vermouth, orange juice, grenadine and rum over the ice. Shake until a frost forms, then pour, without straining, into a highball glass. Decorate with an orange rind spiral and a cocktail cherry.

Bahamas

Serves I

4–5 ice cubes
I measure white rum
I measure Southern Comfort
I measure fresh lemon juice
I dash crème de bananes
thin lemon slice, to decorate

Put the ice cubes in a cocktail shaker and pour in the rum, Southern Comfort, lemon juice and crème de bananes. Shake vigorously, then strain into a chilled cocktail glass. Drop in a thin lemon slice and serve.

Serenade

Serves I

6 ice cubes, crushed
I measure white rum
½ measure Amaretto di Saronno
½ measure coconut cream (see page 17)
2 measures pineapple juice
pineapple slice, to decorate

Put half of the ice in a blender and add the rum, Amaretto, coconut cream and pineapple juice and blend for 20 seconds. Put the remaining ice in a tall glass and pour the cocktail over it. Decorate with a slice of pineapple and drink with a straw.

Discovery Bay

St Lucia

Did you know?

Amaretto is an Italian liqueur, which is said to date back to 1525; it is made from apricot kernels, flavoured with almonds and herbs.

Southern Comfort is a peach-flavoured bourbon whiskey liqueur, which originated in New Orleans.

Pussyfoot

Serves 1
crushed ice
1½ measures white rum
1 measure double cream
1 measure pineapple juice
1 measure lime juice
1 measure cherry juice
to decorate
pineapple slice
cocktail cherry

Put some crushed ice in a blender and add the rum, cream, pineapple juice, lime juice and cherry juice. Blend at high speed for 15–20 seconds, then pour into a hurricane glass. Decorate with a slice of pineapple and a cherry.

Did you know?

Although there is a well-known non-alcoholic cocktail called Pussyfoot, this more potent version, with a generous measure of rum, is something of a lion's paw.

Virgin's Prayer

Serves 2
ice
2 measures light rum
2 measures dark rum
2 measures Kahlúa
2 tablespoons lemon juice
4 tablespoons orange juice
2 lime slices, to decorate

Put some ice in a cocktail shaker and pour in the rums, Kahlúa, lemon juice and orange juice and shake until a frost forms. Strain the cocktail into 2 highball glasses and decorate with the slices of lime.

Bombay Smash

Serves 1
5 ice cubes, crushed
1 measure dark rum
1 measure Malibu
3 measures pineapple juice
2 teaspoons lemon juice
¼ measure Cointreau
to decorate
pineapple cubes
lemon slice

Put half of the ice in a cocktail shaker. Add the rum, Malibu, pineapple juice, lemon juice and Cointreau. Shake until a frost forms. Put the remaining ice in a tall glass and strain the cocktail over it. Decorate with the pineapple cubes and lemon slice and drink with a straw.

Tropical Dream

Serves 1
1 measure white rum
1 measure Midori
1 tablespoon coconut cream (see page 17)
1 tablespoon pineapple juice
3 tablespoons orange juice
3–4 ice cubes
½ measure crème de bananes
½ fresh banana
banana wedge, unpeeled, to decorate

Pour the white rum, Midori, coconut cream, pineapple juice, orange juice and the ice cubes into a blender. Blend for about 10 seconds. Add the crème de bananes and the fresh banana and blend for a further 10 seconds. Decorate with the wedge of banana and drink with a straw.

Pussyfoot

Tropical Dream

Punches and Fizzes

Take the taste buds on a trip around the Deep South and the Caribbean with these long, cooling thirst-quenchers. Visit Havana Beach, pack a Mississippi Punch or make Tobago Fizz.

Florida Skies

Serves I
cracked ice
I measure white rum
¼ measure lime juice
½ measure pineapple juice
soda water, to top up
cucumber or lime slices, to decorate

Put some cracked ice in a tall glass. Pour the rum, lime juice and pineapple juice into a cocktail shaker. Shake lightly. Strain into the glass and top up with soda water. Decorate with slices of cucumber or lime.

Variations
For a Florida Hurricane, add I measure Curaçao and substitute orange juice for the pineapple juice. For a Florida, add ½ measure crème de menthe and decorate with a mint sprig.

Cuba Libre

Serves I
2–3 ice cubes
I½ measures dark rum
juice of ½ lime
Coca Cola, to top up
lime slice, to decorate

Place the ice cubes in a tall tumbler and pour in the rum and lime juice. Stir to mix. Top up with Coca Cola, decorate with a lime slice and drink through a straw.

Mississippi Punch

Serves I
crushed ice
3 drops Angostura bitters
I teaspoon sugar syrup (see page 4)
juice of I lemon
I measure brandy
I measure dark rum
2 measures bourbon or Scotch whisky

Fill a highball glass with crushed ice. Shake the bitters over the ice and pour in the sugar syrup and lemon juice. Stir gently to mix thoroughly. Add the brandy, rum and whisky, in that order, stir once and serve with straws.

Havana Beach

Serves I
½ lime
2 measures pineapple juice
I measure white rum
I teaspoon sugar
ginger ale, to top up
lime slice, to decorate

Cut the lime into 4 pieces and place in a blender with the pineapple juice, rum and sugar. Blend until smooth. Pour into a hurricane glass or large goblet and top up with ginger ale. Decorate with a lime slice.

Did you know?
A hurricane glass is so-called because it is shaped like a hurricane lamp. It is ideal for serving long drinks.

Florida Skies

Havana Beach

Tobago Fizz

Serves 1

4–5 ice cubes
juice of ½ lime or lemon
juice of ½ orange
3 measures golden rum
1 measure single cream
½ teaspoon sugar syrup (see page 4)
soda water, to top up
to decorate
orange slice
strawberry slice

Put the ice cubes in a cocktail shaker. Pour the lime or lemon juice, orange juice, rum, cream and sugar syrup over the ice and shake until a frost forms, then strain into a goblet. Top up with soda water and serve decorated with slices of orange and strawberry speared on a cocktail stick, and drink with straws.

New Orleans Dandy

Serves 1

crushed ice
1 measure light rum
½ measure peach brandy
1 dash orange juice
1 dash lime juice
Champagne, to top up

Place the crushed ice in a cocktail shaker with the rum, peach brandy, orange juice and lime juice. Shake until a frost forms. Strain into a large wine glass and top up with Champagne.

Bahamas Punch

Serves 1

juice of 1 lemon
1 teaspoon sugar syrup (see page 4)
3 drops Angostura bitters
½ teaspoon grenadine
3 measures white or golden rum
orange slice
lemon slice
cracked ice
grated nutmeg, to decorate

Pour the lemon juice and sugar syrup into a mixing glass. Shake in the bitters, then add the grenadine, rum and slices of orange and lemon. Stir thoroughly and chill in the refrigerator until very cold. To serve, fill an old-fashioned glass with cracked ice, pour in the punch, without straining, and sprinkle with nutmeg.

Variation
For a Planter's Punch, substitute lime juice for the lemon juice, a slice of lime for the lemon slice, increase the quantity of grenadine to 1 teaspoon and use dark rum.

Pink Rum

Serves 1

3 drops Angostura bitters
3–4 ice cubes
2 measures white rum
2 measures cranberry juice
1 measure soda water
lime slice, to decorate

Shake the bitters into a highball glass and swirl them around. Add the ice cubes, then pour in the rum, cranberry juice and soda water and serve decorated with a lime slice.

Tobago Fizz

Bahamas Punch

Pink Rum

Golden Rum Punch

Serves 20
50 g (2 oz) sugar
1 litre (1¾ pints) pineapple juice
juice of 6 oranges
juice of 6 lemons
1 bottle golden rum
ice
1 litre (1¾ pints) ginger ale or soda water
to decorate
slices of fruit in season, such as pineapple,
  oranges, cherries and strawberries

Put the sugar in a punch bowl, pour in the pineapple juice and stir to dissolve the sugar. Add the orange and lemon juices and pour in the golden rum. Stir to mix. Put a large block of ice in the punch bowl and leave the punch to become really cold.

When you are ready to serve, pour in the ginger ale or soda water. Decorate with slices of pineapple and orange, cherries, strawberries and any other fruit in season.

Pink Treasure

Serves 1
2 cracked ice cubes
1 measure white rum
1 measure cherry brandy
bitter lemon or soda water
lemon rind spiral, to decorate

Put the ice cubes, rum and cherry brandy in a small glass. Add a splash of bitter lemon or soda water and decorate with the spiral of lemon rind.

Punch Julien

Serves 1
juice of 2 limes
1 measure pineapple juice
3 drops Angostura bitters
½ teaspoon grenadine
1 measure golden rum
3 measures dark rum
lime slice
lemon slice
orange slice
cracked ice
to decorate
grated nutmeg
pineapple wedge

Pour the lime juice and pineapple juice into a mixing glass and shake in the bitters. Pour in the grenadine and golden and dark rums and add the fruit. Stir thoroughly, then chill in the refrigerator for 3 hours. Fill an old-fashioned glass with cracked ice. Pour the punch over the ice and add the fruit. Sprinkle with nutmeg and serve decorated with a pineapple wedge.

Golden Rum Punch

Punch Julien

Slow Sippers

Discover an unimaginable depth of flavour with these rich and potent mixtures. Relax with a Black Widow or warm up with a hot Island Cream Grog.

Alexander Baby

Serves 1
4–5 ice cubes
2 measures dark rum
1 measure crème de cacao
½ measure double cream
grated nutmeg, to decorate

Put the ice cubes in a cocktail shaker and pour the rum, crème de cacao and cream over them. Shake until a frost forms, then strain the drink into a chilled cocktail glass. Sprinkle a little grated nutmeg on top.

Did you know?
Crème de cacao is a chocolate-flavoured liqueur, which comes in colourless and chocolate-brown varieties.

Rum Martini

Serves 1
4–5 ice cubes
1 measure dry vermouth
3 measures white rum
piece of lemon rind

Put the ice cubes in a mixing glass. Pour the vermouth and rum over the ice, stir vigorously, then strain into a chilled cocktail glass. Twist the lemon rind over the drink and drop it in.

Batiste

Serves 1
4–5 ice cubes
1 measure Grand Marnier
2 measures golden or dark rum

Put the ice cubes in a mixing glass. Pour the Grand Marnier and rum over the ice, stir vigorously, then strain into a cocktail glass.

Honeysuckle

Serves 1
4–5 ice cubes
2 measures golden rum
juice of 1 lime
1 teaspoon clear honey

Put the ice cubes in a cocktail shaker. Pour in the rum and lime juice and add the honey. Shake until a frost forms, then strain into a cocktail glass.

Variation
This cocktail is especially flavoursome when made with lemon or orange blossom honey.

Black Widow

Serves 1
4–5 ice cubes
2 measures dark rum
1 measure Southern Comfort
juice of ½ lime
1 dash sugar syrup (see page 4)
lime slice, to decorate

Put the ice in a cocktail shaker. Pour in the rum, Southern Comfort, lime juice and sugar syrup and shake until a frost forms. Strain into a chilled cocktail glass and decorate with a slice of lime.

Alexander Baby

The Alexander family

The Alexander Baby is the younger — but no less powerful — brother of the classic gin- and brandy-based cocktails, the Alexander and Brandy Alexander.

Batiste

Black Widow

Heartwarmer

Serves 12
200 ml (7 fl oz) red grape juice
250 g (8 oz) brown sugar
350 ml (12 fl oz) dark rum
1.5 litres (2½ pints) dry white wine
450 ml (¾ pint) red wine

Put the grape juice in a saucepan, add the sugar and stir over a gentle heat until the sugar has dissolved completely. Stir in the dark rum and set aside. Pour the white wine and red wine into a large saucepan and heat until hot, but not boiling. Add the rum and grape juice mixture and stir together. Serve hot.

White Witch

Serves 1
8–10 ice cubes
1 measure white rum
½ measure white crème de cacao
½ measure Cointreau
juice of ½ lime
soda water, to top up
to decorate
orange slice
lime slice

Put 4–5 ice cubes in a cocktail shaker and pour in the white rum, crème de cacao, Cointreau and lime juice. Put 4–5 fresh ice cubes in an old-fashioned glass. Shake the drink, then strain it into the glass. Top up with soda water and stir to mix. Decorate with slices of orange and lime and serve with straws.

Tip
If you roll whole limes around quite hard on a board with your hand, you will find that you get more juice from them.

Between the Sheets

Serves 1
4–5 ice cubes
1¼ measures brandy
1 measure white rum
½ measure Cointreau
¾ measure lemon juice
½ measure sugar syrup (see page 4)

Put the ice cubes in a cocktail shaker. Add the brandy, white rum, Cointreau, lemon juice and sugar syrup and shake until a frost forms. Strain into a chilled cocktail glass.

Sunset Tea

Serves 2
200 ml (7 fl oz) freshly brewed Indian tea
½ measure golden rum
1 measure Cointreau
2 measures orange juice
to decorate
2 orange slices, each stuck with 3 cloves
cinnamon sticks

Pour the tea into 2 heatproof glasses. Put the rum, Cointreau and orange juice in a small saucepan. Place it over a low heat and bring the mixture to just under boiling point, stirring constantly. Pour immediately into the glasses with the tea. Decorate each one with a slice of orange stuck with 3 cloves, and a cinnamon stick.

Island Cream Grog

Serves 1
2 measures rum
200 ml (7 fl oz) boiling water
sugar, to taste
whipped cream
grated nutmeg

Warm a heatproof glass with a handle and pour in the rum and boiling water. Add sugar to taste and stir. Spoon some whipped cream on the top and sprinkle with grated nutmeg.

Variation
To make a Hot Buttered Rum, stir 15 g (½ oz) butter with the rum before adding the boiling water and omit the whipped cream.

White Witch

Sunset Tea

Island Cream Grog

Gin Cocktails

TIMELESS CLASSICS

DRY MARTINI 38

CLOVER CLUB 38

NEW ORLEANS DRY MARTINI 38

HORSE'S NECK 38

OPERA 38

PINK CLOVER CLUB 40

ALBEMARLE FIZZ 40

BRONX 40

WHITE LADY 40

MAIDEN'S PRAYER 42

FRENCH '75 42

MONKEY GLAND 42

PARADISE 42

ORANGE BLOSSOM 42

RICH AND RARE

CROSSBOW 44

GIN TROPICAL 44

LONG ISLAND ICED TEA 44

GOLDEN DAWN 44

JULIANA BLUE 46

CHERRY JULEP 46

BIJOU 46

NIGHT OF PASSION 46

SAPPHIRE MARTINI 48

PEACH BLOW 48

HONOLULU 48

BEN'S ORANGE CREAM 48

COOLERS AND FIZZERS

GIN SLING 50

GIN CUP 50

GIN COOLER 50

GIN FLORADORA 50

SEA BREEZE 52

MORNING GLORY FIZZ 52

SYDNEY FIZZ 52

GIN FIX 52

SINGAPORE GIN SLING 52

SALTY DOG 54

HONEYDEW 54

LIME GIN FIZZ 54

JOHN COLLINS 54

PINK GIN 54

HIGH SPIRITS

COLLINSON 56

ALICE SPRINGS 56

POET'S DREAM 56

MOON RIVER 56

RED KISS 58

KNOCKOUT 58

KISS IN THE DARK 58

EARTHQUAKE 58

BURNSIDES 60

LUIGI 60

WOODSTOCK 60

STORMY WEATHER 60

Gin

Gin is a clear grain spirit, further distilled with a variety of herb and fruit flavourings – the botanicals – which has been produced commercially for over 400 years. Originally from Holland, it has had a chequered social career, sinking to the lowest social depths in eighteenth-century London, when it was distilled from anything that would ferment, before rising to a respected place among the mixed drinks of the Victorian age – the fizzes, fixes and slings – and later among the strong, potent mixes of the cocktail age of the 1920s.

Which Gin to Choose

Gins of previous centuries would not be to the taste of present-day gin drinkers, for they were strongly flavoured and very sweet. During the nineteenth century, London gained a reputation for its dry gin, which was distilled from the pure water from villages then on the edge of the countryside, such as Clerkenwell and Finsbury. London dry gin is now a generic term for unsweetened dry gin and, although it can be made anywhere in the world, some countries will only permit the description 'London dry' if the gin is imported from the United Kingdom. Plymouth gin, which can be made only in Plymouth, is a more aromatic, slightly sweetened gin. It has always been held in great affection by the Royal Navy, which has a tradition that true Pink Gin must be made with Plymouth gin. Dutch gin (which may be labelled Holland's or Geneva) has a fuller flavour still. It is usually drunk neat and very cold, ad is not suitable for making cocktails. Sloe gin (gin flavoured with sloes and sugar) is a bright clear red colour, and is delicious as an after-dinner drink.

Relative Strengths

The flavour of gin varies subtly from one brand to the next. It is also important when choosing a gin to look closely at the label. Some types are lower in alcohol than others (they range in percentage volume from 47.3 to 37.5%), resulting in a less potent drink. All alcoholic drinks contain congeners (the elements in alcohol that cause hangovers). There are fewer of these in colourless spirits such as vodka than in spirits like rum, and fewest of all in gin.

The Ideal Cocktail Base

Gin makes an ideal base for cocktails because it blends well with other flavours, whets the appetite rather than dulling it and gives the drinker an instant lift. It is not for nothing that the most famous cocktail of all time – the Dry Martini – is a gin-based drink. Famous Dry Martini drinkers include Noel Coward, Humphrey Bogart, W C Fields, Dean Martin and Ernest Hemingway.

Lime Gin Fizz
(see page 54)

Timeless Classics

This selection comprises a dazzling collection of drinks, many of which date back to the 1920s, including some of the most exciting gin cocktails yet devised.

Dry Martini

Serves 1
5–6 ice cubes
½ measure dry vermouth
3 measures gin
1 green olive

Put the ice cubes in a mixing glass. Pour the vermouth and gin over the ice and stir (never shake) vigorously and evenly without splashing, then strain into a chilled cocktail glass. Serve with a green olive.

Clover Club

Serves 1
4–5 ice cubes
juice of 1 lime
½ teaspoon sugar syrup (see page 4)
1 egg white
3 measures gin
to decorate
grated lime rind
lime wedge

Put the ice cubes in a cocktail shaker. Pour the lime juice, sugar syrup, egg white and gin over the ice and shake until a frost forms. Strain into a tumbler and serve decorated with grated lime rind and a lime wedge.

New Orleans Dry Martini

Serves 1
5–6 ice cubes
2–3 drops pernod
1 measure dry vermouth
4 measures gin

Put the ice cubes in a mixing glass. Pour the pernod over the ice, then pour in the vermouth and gin. Stir (never shake) vigorously and evenly without splashing, then strain into a chilled cocktail glass.

Horse's Neck

Serves 1
4–6 cracked ice cubes
1½ measures gin
dry ginger ale, to top up
lemon rind spiral, to decorate

Put the ice in a tall glass and pour in the gin. Top up with dry ginger ale then dangle the lemon rind over the edge of the glass.

Variation
This classic cocktail can also be made with a brandy, rum or whisky base instead of gin. The lemon rind spiral is essential.

Opera

Serves 1
4–5 ice cubes
1 measure Dubonnet
½ measure Curaçao
2 measures gin
orange rind spiral, to decorate

Put the ice cubes in a mixing glass. Pour the Dubonnet, Curaçao and gin over the ice. Stir evenly, then strain into a chilled cocktail glass. Decorate with the orange rind spiral and serve.

Dry Martini

Clover Club

Opera

Did you know?

The Dry Martini, which was invented at the Knickerbocker Hotel in New York in 1910, has become the most famous cocktail of all time. Lemon rind is sometimes used as a decoration instead of a green olive.

Pink Clover Club

Serves 1

4–5 ice cubes
juice of 1 lime
1 dash grenadine
1 egg white
3 measures gin
strawberry slice, to decorate

Put the ice cubes in a cocktail shaker. Pour the lime juice, grenadine, egg white and gin over the ice. Shake until a frost forms, then strain into a cocktail glass. Decorate with a strawberry slice and serve with a straw.

Albemarle Fizz

Serves 1

4–6 ice cubes
1 measure gin
juice of ½ lemon
2 dashes raspberry syrup
½ teaspoon sugar syrup (see page 4)
soda water, to top up
2 cocktail cherries, to decorate

Put 2–3 ice cubes in a mixing glass and add the gin, lemon juice, raspberry syrup and sugar syrup. Stir to mix then strain into a highball glass. Add 2–3 fresh ice cubes and top up with soda water. Decorate with 2 cherries on a cocktail stick and serve with straws.

Bronx

Serves 1

cracked ice
1 measure gin
1 measure sweet vermouth
1 measure dry vermouth
2 measures fresh orange juice

Place some cracked ice, the gin, sweet and dry vermouths and orange juice in a cocktail shaker. Shake to mix. Pour into a small glass, straining the drink if preferred.

White Lady

Serves 1

3–4 ice cubes
2 measures gin
1 measure Cointreau
1 teaspoon lemon juice
about ½ teaspoon egg white
lemon rind spiral, to decorate

Place the ice cubes, gin, Cointreau, lemon juice and egg white in a cocktail shaker. Shake to mix then strain into a cocktail glass. Decorate with the spiral of lemon rind.

Variation

To transform a White Lady into a Pink Lady, substitute 1 teaspoon grenadine for the Cointreau.

Pink Clover Club

White Lady

Maiden's Prayer
Serves 1
4–5 ice cubes
3 drops Angostura bitters
juice of 1 lemon
1 measure Cointreau
2 measures gin

Put the ice cubes in a cocktail shaker. Pour the bitters over the ice, add the lemon juice, Cointreau and gin and shake until a frost forms. Strain into a cocktail glass and serve with a straw.

French '75
Serves 1
cracked ice
1 measure gin
juice of ½ lemon
1 teaspoon caster sugar
chilled Champagne or sparkling dry white wine, to top up
orange slice, to decorate

Half-fill a tall glass with cracked ice. Add the gin, lemon juice and sugar and stir well. Top up with chilled Champagne or sparkling dry white wine and serve with an orange slice.

Monkey Gland
Serves 1
1 measure orange juice
2 measures gin
3 dashes pernod
3 dashes grenadine
3–4 ice cubes

Put the orange juice, gin, pernod and grenadine in a cocktail shaker with 3–4 ice cubes. Shake well then strain into a chilled cocktail glass.

Paradise
Serves 1
2–3 cracked ice cubes
1 measure gin
½ measure apricot brandy
½ measure fresh orange juice
1 dash fresh lemon juice
to decorate
orange slice
lemon slice

Place the ice cubes in a cocktail shaker and add the gin, apricot brandy and orange and lemon juices. Shake to mix then strain into a cocktail glass. Decorate with the orange and lemon slices.

Orange Blossom
Serves 1
1 measure gin
1 measure sweet vermouth
1 measure fresh orange juice
2–3 ice cubes
orange slices, to decorate

Pour the gin, sweet vermouth and orange juice into a cocktail shaker and shake to mix. Place the ice cubes in a tumbler and strain the cocktail over them. Decorate the rim of the glass with orange slices.

Maiden's Prayer

French '75

Did you know?

Orange Blossom is a cocktail from the Prohibition years, when it was also known as an Adirondack. The orange juice could disguise a hearty slug of rotgut gin.

Rich and Rare

With fantastic ingredients, such as the sapphire-coloured blue Curaçao, these exotic combinations make a wonderful collection of gin spectaculars.

Crossbow

Serves 1
4–5 ice cubes
½ measure gin
½ measure crème de cacao
½ measure Cointreau
drinking chocolate powder, to decorate

Put the ice cubes in a cocktail shaker and add the gin, crème de cacao and Cointreau. Dampen the rim of a chilled cocktail glass with a little water then dip the rim into a saucer of drinking chocolate. Shake the drink vigorously then strain into the prepared glass.

Gin Tropical

Serves 1
4–6 ice cubes
1½ measures gin
1 measure fresh lemon juice
1 measure passion fruit juice
½ measure fresh orange juice
soda water, to top up
orange rind spiral, to decorate

Put 2–3 ice cubes in a cocktail shaker, pour in the gin, lemon juice, passion fruit juice and orange juice and shake well. Put 2–3 fresh ice cubes in an old-fashioned glass and strain the cocktail over the ice. Top up with soda water and stir gently. Decorate with an orange rind spiral.

Long Island Iced Tea

Serves 1
8 ice cubes
½ measure gin
½ measure vodka
½ measure white rum
½ measure tequila
½ measure Cointreau
1 measure lemon juice
½ teaspoon sugar syrup (see page 4)
Coca Cola, to top up
lemon slice, to decorate

Put 2 ice cubes in a mixing glass. Add the gin, vodka, rum, tequila, Cointreau, lemon juice and sugar syrup. Stir well, then strain into a tall glass almost filled with the remaining ice cubes. Top up with Coca Cola and decorate with the slice of lemon.

Golden Dawn

Serves 1
4–5 ice cubes
juice of ½ orange
1 measure Calvados
1 measure apricot brandy
3 measures gin
soda water, to top up
skewered orange rind, to decorate

Put the ice cubes in a cocktail shaker. Pour the orange juice, Calvados, apricot brandy and gin over the ice and shake until a frost forms. Strain into a highball glass, top up with soda water and decorate with orange rind.

Crossbow

Gin Tropical

Juliana Blue

Serves 1
crushed ice
1 measure gin
½ measure Cointreau
½ measure blue Curaçao
2 measures pineapple juice
½ measure fresh lime juice
1 measure coconut cream (see page 17)
1–2 ice cubes
to decorate
pineapple slice
cocktail cherries

Put some crushed ice in a blender and pour in the gin, Cointreau, blue Curaçao, pineapple and lime juices and coconut cream. Blend at high speed for several seconds until the mixture has the consistency of soft snow. Put the ice cubes in a cocktail glass and strain the mixture on to them. Decorate with a pineapple slice and cocktail cherries. Serve with straws.

Cherry Julep

Serves 1
3–4 ice cubes
juice of ½ lemon
1 teaspoon sugar syrup (see page 4)
1 teaspoon grenadine
1 measure cherry brandy
1 measure sloe gin
2 measures gin
chopped ice
lemon rind strips, to decorate

Put the ice cubes in a cocktail shaker. Pour the lemon juice, sugar syrup, grenadine, cherry brandy, sloe gin and gin over the ice. Fill a highball glass with finely chopped ice. Shake the mixture until a frost forms then strain it into the ice-filled glass. Decorate with lemon rind strips and serve.

Bijou

Serves 1
3 cracked ice cubes
1 measure gin
½ measure green Chartreuse
½ measure sweet vermouth
1 dash orange bitters
to decorate
green olive
piece of lemon rind

Put the ice cubes in a mixing glass and add the gin, Chartreuse, vermouth and bitters. Stir well and strain into a cocktail glass. Place the olive on a cocktail stick and add to the cocktail then squeeze the oil from the lemon rind over the surface of the cocktail.

Night of Passion

Serves 1
2 measures gin
1 measure Cointreau
1 tablespoon fresh lemon juice
2 measures peach nectar
2 tablespoons passion fruit juice
6–8 ice cubes

Put the gin, Cointreau, lemon juice, peach nectar and passion fruit juice in a cocktail shaker with 3–4 ice cubes and shake well. Strain into an old-fashioned glass over 3–4 fresh ice cubes.

Juliana Blue

Chartreuse, a secret recipe

Chartreuse is made by the Carthusian monks at their monastery near Grenoble, in the French Alps. The recipe is a secret but it is known to contain over 130 different herbs. There are two versions: green which is the stronger, and the weaker but sweeter yellow.

Cherry Julep

Sapphire Martini

Serves 1
4 ice cubes
2 measures gin
½ measure blue Curaçao
1 red or blue cocktail cherry (optional)

Put the ice cubes in a cocktail shaker. Pour in the gin and blue Curaçao. Shake well to mix. Strain into a cocktail glass and carefully drop in a cocktail cherry, if using.

Peach Blow

Serves 1
8 cracked ice cubes
juice of ½ lemon
4 strawberries, crushed
1½ teaspoons caster sugar
1 tablespoon double cream
2 measures gin
soda water, to top up
strawberry slices, to decorate

Put 4 of the ice cubes in a cocktail shaker, add the lemon juice, strawberries, sugar, double cream and gin and shake well. Strain into a tall glass and top up with soda water. Decorate with strawberry slices.

Did you know?

This recipe is quite deceptive. Despite its name, it is actually an alcoholic version of strawberries and cream.

Honolulu

Serves 1
4–5 ice cubes
1 measure pineapple juice
1 measure fresh lemon juice
1 measure fresh orange juice
½ teaspoon grenadine
3 measures gin
to decorate
pineapple slice
cocktail cherry

Put the ice cubes in a cocktail shaker. Pour the pineapple, lemon and orange juices, the grenadine and gin over the ice and shake until a frost forms. Strain the drink into a chilled cocktail glass and decorate with the pineapple slice and cherry.

Ben's Orange Cream

Serves 1
4–5 ice cubes
1 measure Cointreau
1 measure single cream
3 measures gin
1 tablespoon sugar syrup (see page 4)
chocolate flake, to decorate

Put the ice cubes in a cocktail shaker. Pour the Cointreau, cream and gin over the ice. Add the sugar syrup to the gin mixture and shake until a frost forms. Pour into a large glass and decorate with a chocolate flake.

Sapphire Martini

Honolulu

Ben's Orange Cream

Coolers and Fizzers

These long refreshing drinks, such as the Sea Breeze and the Morning Glory Fizz, will cool and invigorate on a hot summer's evening.

Gin Sling

Serves 1

4–5 ice cubes
juice of ½ lemon
1 measure cherry brandy
3 measures gin
soda water, to top up
stemmed cherries, to decorate (optional)

Put the ice cubes in a cocktail shaker. Pour the lemon juice, cherry brandy and gin over the ice and shake until a frost forms. Pour without straining into a hurricane glass and top up with soda water. Decorate with cherries, if liked, and serve with straws.

Gin Cup

Serves 1

3 mint sprigs, plus extra to decorate
1 teaspoon sugar syrup (see page 4)
chopped ice
juice of ½ lemon
3 measures gin

Put the mint and sugar syrup in an old-fashioned glass and stir them about to bruise the mint slightly. Fill the glass with chopped ice, add the lemon juice and gin and stir until a frost begins to form. Decorate with extra mint sprigs.

Gin Cooler

Serves 1

3–4 ice cubes
½ teaspoon grenadine
juice of 1 lemon
3 measures gin
soda water, to top up
to decorate
1 cocktail cherry
1 lemon slice

Put the ice cubes in a highball glass. Pour the grenadine over the ice, then the lemon juice and the gin and stir evenly allowing the mixture to blend. Top up the drink with soda water. Decorate with a cherry and a lemon slice.

Gin Floradora

Serves 1

4–5 ice cubes
½ teaspoon sugar syrup (see page 4)
juice of ½ lime
½ teaspoon grenadine
2 measures gin
dry ginger ale, to top up
lime rind spiral, to decorate

Put the ice cubes in a cocktail shaker. Pour in the sugar syrup, lime juice, grenadine and gin and shake until a frost forms. Pour without straining into a hurricane glass. Top up with dry ginger ale, decorate with a lime rind spiral and serve.

Gin Sling

in Cup

Sea Breeze

Serves 1

6–8 ice cubes
½ measure fresh grapefruit juice
½ measure cranberry juice
1 measure dry vermouth
3 measures gin
lime slice, to decorate

Put 2–3 ice cubes in a mixing glass. Pour the grapefruit juice, cranberry juice, vermouth and gin over the ice then stir gently. Put 4–5 fresh ice cubes in a chilled hurricane glass and strain the cocktail over the ice. Decorate with a lime slice.

Morning Glory Fizz

Serves 1

4–5 ice cubes
1 measure fresh lemon juice
½ teaspoon sugar syrup (see page 4)
3 measures gin
1 egg white
3 drops pernod
ginger ale, to top up

Put the ice cubes in a cocktail shaker. Pour the lemon juice, sugar syrup and gin over the ice. Add the egg white, then the pernod and shake until a frost forms. Strain the cocktail into a chilled old-fashioned glass, top up with ginger ale and serve with a straw.

Variation
The Morning Glory Fizz can be made with whisky instead of gin.

Sydney Fizz

Serves 1

4–5 ice cubes
1 measure fresh lemon juice
1 measure fresh orange juice
½ teaspoon grenadine
3 measures gin
soda water, to top up
orange slice, to decorate

Put the ice cubes in a cocktail shaker. Pour the lemon and orange juices, grenadine and gin over the ice and shake vigorously until a frost forms. Strain into an old-fashioned glass. Top up with soda water, add the orange slice and serve.

Gin Fix

Serves 1

crushed ice
1 tablespoon caster sugar
juice of ¼ lemon
1 measure water
2 measures gin
orange and lemon slices, to decorate

Fill a tall glass two-thirds full with crushed ice. Add the sugar, lemon juice, water and gin and stir well. Decorate the rim of the glass with orange and lemon slices.

Singapore Gin Sling

Serves 1

6–8 ice cubes
juice of ½ lemon
juice of ½ orange
1 measure cherry brandy
3 measures gin
3 drops Angostura bitters
soda water, to top up
1 lemon slice, to decorate

Put 4–6 ice cubes in a cocktail shaker. Pour the lemon and orange juices, cherry brandy and gin over the ice and add the bitters. Shake the mixture until a frost forms. Put 2 fresh ice cubes in a hurricane glass. Strain the cocktail into the glass and top up with soda water. Decorate with the lemon slice and serve.

Sea Breeze

Singapore Gin Sling

Morning Glory Fizz

Did you know?
Fixes are also known as Daisies. They often contain large quantities of fruit or have lavish fruit decorations.

Salty Dog
Serves 1

2–3 ice cubes
pinch of salt
1 measure gin
2–2½ measures fresh grapefruit juice
orange slice, to decorate

Put the ice cubes in an old-fashioned glass. Put the salt on the ice and add the gin and grapefruit juice. Stir gently and serve. Decorate with an orange slice.

Variation
A Salty Dog can also be made with vodka (see page 70). Sometimes the glass is rimmed with salt, like a Margarita.

Honeydew
Serves 1

1 measure gin
½ measure fresh lemon juice
1 dash pernod
50 g (2 oz) honeydew melon, diced
3–4 cracked ice cubes
Champagne, to top up

Place the gin, lemon juice, pernod and diced melon in a blender and blend for 30 seconds, then pour into a large wine glass over cracked ice. Top up with Champagne.

Did you know?
This is the drink to serve at the end of a late Sunday brunch – the combination of honeydew melon and gin makes the perfect transition from breakfast to lunchtime drinks.

Lime Gin Fizz
Serves 1

4–5 ice cubes
2 measures gin
1 measure lime cordial
soda water, to top up
lime wedges, to decorate

Put the ice cubes in a tall glass. Pour the gin and the lime cordial over the ice cubes. Top up with soda water, decorate with wedges of lime and serve with straws.

John Collins
Serves 1

5–6 ice cubes
1 teaspoon sugar syrup (see page 4)
1 measure fresh lemon juice
3 measures gin
soda water, to top up
to decorate
lemon slice
mint sprig

Put the ice cubes in a cocktail shaker. Pour in the sugar syrup, lemon juice and gin and shake vigorously until a frost forms. Pour without straining into a Collins glass. Add the lemon slice and the mint sprig and top up with soda water. Stir gently and serve.

Pink Gin
Serves 1

1–4 dashes Angostura bitters
1 measure gin
iced water, to top up

Shake the bitters into a cocktail glass and roll it around until the sides are well coated. Add the gin, then top up with iced water to taste.

Did you know?
Angostura bitters were originally intended for medicinal use, to combat malaria, but the Royal Navy put this herb-flavoured essence in glasses of gin, thus inventing Pink Gin. Using orange bitters instead of Angostura transforms the drink into a Yellow Gin.

Salty Dog

Lime Gin Fizz

Tall story

The Collins is the tallest of the mixed drinks. It is made with a spirit, lemon juice and water. The John Collins, originally made with Holland's gin, was the first. Now there are also the Mick Collins (Irish whiskey), Pierre Collins (cognac) and the Pedro Collins (rum).

High Spirits

From the Knockout and the Earthquake to the Kiss in the Dark and Stormy Weather, these are serious cocktails, so watch your step!

Collinson

Serves 1

3 cracked ice cubes
1 dash orange bitters
1 measure gin
½ measure dry vermouth
¼ measure kirsch
piece of lemon rind
to decorate
½ strawberry
lemon slice

Put the ice cubes in a mixing glass, then add the orange bitters, gin, vermouth and kirsch. Stir well and strain into a cocktail glass. Squeeze the oil from the lemon rind over the surface, and decorate the rim of the glass with the strawberry and lemon slice.

Poet's Dream

Serves 1

4–5 ice cubes
1 measure Bénédictine
1 measure dry vermouth
3 measures gin
piece of lemon rind

Put the ice cubes in a mixing glass. Pour the Bénédictine, vermouth and gin over the ice and stir vigorously, without splashing. Strain into a chilled cocktail glass. Twist the lemon rind over the drink, drop it in and serve.

Alice Springs

Serves 1

4–5 ice cubes
1 measure fresh lemon juice
1 measure fresh orange juice
½ teaspoon grenadine
3 measures gin
3 drops Angostura bitters
soda water, to top up
orange slice, to decorate

Put the ice cubes in a cocktail shaker. Pour in the lemon juice, orange juice, grenadine and gin. Add the bitters and shake until a frost forms. Pour into a tall glass and top up with soda water. Decorate with an orange slice and serve with straws.

Moon River

Serves 4

4–5 ice cubes
½ measure dry gin
½ measure apricot brandy
½ measure Cointreau
¼ measure Galliano
¼ measure fresh lemon juice
cocktail cherry, to decorate

Put some ice cubes in a mixing glass and pour in the gin, apricot brandy, Cointreau, Galliano and lemon juice. Stir then strain the drink into a large chilled cocktail glass. Decorate with the cherry and serve.

Collinson

Did you know?
Bénédictine has been made for almost 500 years, originally by the monks of Fécamp Abbey in Normandy. When mixed with an equal quantity of brandy it is known as a B&B.

Alice Springs

Red Kiss
Serves I
3 cracked ice cubes
I measure dry vermouth
½ measure gin
½ measure cherry brandy
to decorate
cocktail cherry
lemon rind spiral

Put the ice cubes in a mixing glass, add the vermouth, gin and cherry brandy and stir well. Strain into a chilled cocktail glass and decorate with the cherry and a lemon rind spiral.

Knockout
Serves I
4–5 ice cubes
I measure dry vermouth
½ measure white crème de menthe
2 measures gin
I drop pernod
lemon slice, to serve

Put the ice cubes in a mixing glass. Pour the vermouth, crème de menthe and gin over the ice, stir vigorously, then strain into a chilled old-fashioned glass. Add the pernod and serve with a lemon slice.

Kiss in the Dark
Serves I
4–5 ice cubes
I measure gin
I measure cherry brandy
I teaspoon dry vermouth

Put the ice cubes in a cocktail shaker and pour in the gin, cherry brandy and dry vermouth. Shake then strain into a chilled cocktail glass.

Earthquake
Serves I
6–8 ice cubes
I measure gin
I measure whisky
I measure pernod

Put 3–4 ice cubes in a cocktail shaker. Add the gin, whisky and pernod and shake well. Strain into a cocktail glass and add 3–4 fresh ice cubes.
Did you know?
This cocktail is an extremely potent concoction. Should an earthquake occur while you are drinking it, commented one 1920s cocktail book, it won't matter!

Red Kiss

Knockout

Did you know?

Crème de menthe is a sweetish mint-flavoured liqueur. It may be green or white, although the flavour remains the same. The white version is used in a Knockout to blend with the milky colour of the pernod.

Burnsides

Serves 1

8–10 ice cubes
2 drops Angostura bitters
1 teaspoon cherry brandy
1 measure sweet vermouth
2 measures dry vermouth
2 measures gin
lemon rind strips, to decorate

Put 4–5 ice cubes in a cocktail shaker. Dash the bitters over the ice, add the cherry brandy, sweet and dry vermouths and gin. Shake lightly, then strain into a glass over the remaining ice cubes. Decorate with lemon rind strips.

Luigi

Serves 1

4–5 ice cubes
1 measure fresh orange juice
1 measure dry vermouth
½ measure Cointreau
1 measure grenadine
2 measures gin
blood orange slice, to decorate

Put the ice cubes in a mixing glass. Pour the orange juice, vermouth, Cointreau, grenadine and gin over the ice and stir vigorously. Strain into a chilled cocktail glass, decorate with the orange slice and serve.

Woodstock

Serves 1

2–3 ice cubes, crushed
1 measure gin
1 measure dry vermouth
¼ measure Cointreau
1 measure fresh orange juice
piece of orange rind
orange rind spiral, to decorate

Put the ice in a cocktail shaker and add the gin, vermouth, Cointreau and orange juice. Shake to mix and strain into a cocktail glass. Squeeze the oil from the orange rind over the surface, and decorate with the spiral of orange rind.

Stormy Weather

Serves 1

3 cracked ice cubes
1½ measures gin
¼ measure Mandarine Napoléon
¼ measure dry vermouth
¼ measure sweet vermouth
orange rind spiral, to decorate

Put the ice cubes in a cocktail shaker and add the gin, Mandarine Napoléon and dry and sweet vermouths. Shake to mix and strain into a chilled cocktail glass. Decorate the rim of the glass with the spiral of orange rind.

Luigi

Burnsides

Did you know?
Mandarine Napoléon is a French tangerine-flavoured liqueur.

Woodstock

Vodka Cocktails

Vodka

Just as Scotland and Ireland both claim to have invented whisky, so Russia and Poland argue over the origins of vodka. The Poles reckon that they were distilling vodka as early as the eighth century and by the eleventh century, they were producing a medicinal spirit called *gorzalka*, which would be more or less recognizable today as vodka. The first documented production of vodka in Russia dates from the end of the ninth century, although details of the first known distillery, at Khylnovsk, were not recorded until 1174. The word vodka, meaning 'little water', is derived from the Russian *voda* – water – but as it is called *wodka* in Poland, this is an unreliable guide to its origins. In fact, the word vodka was not officially recognized until the end of the nineteenth century, when state distilleries and standard production techniques were introduced in Russia.

The First Exports

The vodka of the distant past was very different from the drink produced today. It was originally distilled from potato mash, traditionally rotting potatoes, and was often flavoured with herbs, spices, honey, fruit, nuts and a variety of aromatics, but later it was also produced from grains, such as wheat, or molasses. The drink dubbed by the British Ambassador in the fourteenth century as 'the Russian national drink', was first exported in 1505, to Sweden. However, it was not until the years following the Bolshevik Revolution that vodka really took off in the West. When the Communists took over the distilleries, many private vodka-makers left Russia. One of them, Smirnoff, travelled to the United States via Paris and, in 1934, the first American vodka distillery was established. Even then, interest in the spirit was limited and it was not until the 'swinging sixties' that vodka became a popular drink among the newly independent younger generation. This coincided with the rediscovery of cocktails, which had gone into something of a decline following World War II.

Modern Vodka

Western vodka is flavourless, colourless and odourless, making it a perfect partner for other spirits and flavourings; it has the additional advantage of leaving no tell-tale signs of drinking on the breath. Vodka cocktails are the younger cousins of the classics based on gin, whisky or brandy that had their heyday during the 1920s, but they have become firm favourites in bars across the world. Things have now gone full circle and it has become trendy to drink flavoured vodkas once again. Some of these modern flavourings, such as chilli, seem bizarre to contemplate and it is difficult to think of many palatable cocktails based on them. However, other traditional flavours, such as orange or peach, could provide an interesting base for a range of popular cocktail recipes.

Because ordinary vodka is so versatile in cocktails, there are plenty of opportunities for experimenting at home to create fascinating new combinations of taste and colour without worrying about spoiling the taste of the base.

Kamikaze (see page 90)

Vodka Classics

The Moscow Mule was arguably the first true vodka cocktail and since its invention in 1941, a complete repertoire of classics has developed from the sophisticated Vodka Gibson to the robust Bloody Mary and from the richly flavoured Black Russian to the refreshing Screwdriver.

Astronaut

Serves 1

8–10 cracked ice cubes
½ measure white rum
½ measure vodka
½ measure fresh lemon juice
1 dash passion fruit juice
lemon wedge, to decorate

Put 4–5 ice cubes in a cocktail shaker and add the rum, vodka, lemon juice and passion fruit juice. Fill an old-fashioned glass with the remaining ice cubes. Shake the cocktail until a frost forms, then strain it into the glass. Decorate with the lemon wedge and serve.

Bloody Mary

Serves 1

4–5 ice cubes
juice of ½ lemon
½ teaspoon horseradish sauce
2 drops Worcestershire sauce
1 drop Tabasco sauce
2 measures thick tomato juice
2 measures vodka
salt and cayenne pepper
to decorate (optional)
celery stick, with the leaves left on
lemon or lime slice

Put the ice cubes in a cocktail shaker. Pour the lemon juice, horseradish sauce, Worcestershire sauce, Tabasco sauce, tomato juice and vodka over the ice. Shake until a frost forms. Pour into a tall glass, add a pinch of salt and a pinch of cayenne pepper and decorate with a celery stick and a lemon or lime slice, if you like.

Le Mans

Serves 1

2–3 cracked ice cubes
1 measure Cointreau
½ measure vodka
soda water, to top up
lemon slice, to decorate

Put the cracked ice in a tall glass. Add the Cointreau and vodka, stir and top up with soda water. Float the lemon slice on the top.

Hair Raiser

Serves 1

1–2 cracked ice cubes
1 measure vodka
1 measure sweet vermouth
1 measure tonic water
lemon and lime rind spirals, to decorate

Put the cracked ice in a tall glass and pour over the vodka, vermouth and tonic. Stir lightly. Decorate with the lemon and lime rind spirals and serve with a straw.

Screwdriver

Serves 1

2–3 ice cubes
1½ measures vodka
freshly squeezed orange juice, to top up

Put the ice cubes in a tumbler. Add the vodka, top up with orange juice and stir lightly.

Astronaut

Bloody Mary

Bloody Mary
variations

There are many variations on this classic cocktail, invented in 1921 at Harry's Bar in Paris. They include the Bloody Maria which is made with tequila (see page 106) and the non-alcoholic Virgin Mary.

Godmother

Serves I

2–3 cracked ice cubes
1½ measures vodka
½ measure Amaretto di Saronno

Put the ice cubes in a tumbler. Add the vodka and Amaretto. Stir lightly and serve.

Variation

To make a Godchild, shake I measure each of vodka, Amaretto and double cream with ice. Strain into a cocktail glass and serve.

Harvey Wallbanger

Serves I

6 ice cubes
I measure vodka
3 measures fresh orange juice
I–2 teaspoons Galliano
orange slices, to decorate

Put half the ice cubes in a cocktail shaker and the remainder in a tall glass. Add the vodka and orange juice to the cocktail shaker. Shake well for about 30 seconds, then strain into the glass. Float the Galliano on top. Decorate with orange slices and serve with straws.

Vodka Sazerac

Serves I

I sugar cube
2 drops Angostura bitters
3 drops pernod
2–3 ice cubes
2 measures vodka
lemonade, to top up

Put the sugar cube in an old-fashioned glass and shake the bitters on to it. Add the pernod and swirl it about so that it clings to the side of the glass. Drop in the ice cubes and pour in the vodka. Top up with lemonade, then stir gently.

Vodka Gibson

Serves I

6 ice cubes
I measure vodka
½ measure dry vermouth
pearl onion (optional)

Put the ice cubes in a cocktail shaker and add the vodka and vermouth. Shake until a frost forms, then strain into a cocktail glass and decorate with the pearl onion on a cocktail stick.

Vodka Collins

Serves I

6 ice cubes
2 measures vodka
juice of I lime
I teaspoon caster sugar
soda water, to top up
to decorate
lemon or lime slices
cocktail cherry

Put half the ice cubes in a cocktail shaker and add the vodka, lime juice and sugar and shake until a frost forms. Strain into a large tumbler, add the remaining ice and top up with soda water. Decorate with lemon or lime slices and a cherry.

Inspiration

Serves I

4–5 ice cubes
½ measure Bénédictine
½ measure dry vermouth
2 measures vodka
lime rind spiral, to decorate

Put the ice cubes in a mixing glass. Pour the Bénédictine, vermouth and vodka over the ice. Stir vigorously, then strain into a chilled cocktail glass and decorate with the lime rind spiral.

Harvey Wallbanger

Vodka Sazerac

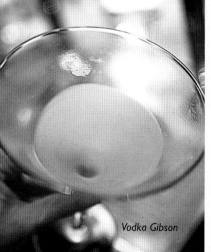

Vodka Gibson

Surfing and Vodka

The Harvey Wallbanger is a cocktail from the 1960s, named after a Californian surfer called Harvey who drank so many Screwdrivers topped with Galliano that, as he tried to find his way out of the bar, he banged and bounced from one wall to the other.

Xantippe
Serves I
4–5 ice cubes
I measure cherry brandy
I measure yellow Chartreuse
2 measures vodka

Put the ice cubes in a mixing glass. Pour the cherry brandy, yellow Chartreuse and vodka over the ice and stir vigorously. Strain into a chilled cocktail glass.

Iceberg
Serves I
4–6 ice cubes
I½ measures vodka
I dash pernod

Put the ice cubes in an old-fashioned glass. Pour in the vodka and add the pernod.

Haven
Serves I
2–3 ice cubes
I tablespoon grenadine
I measure pernod
I measure vodka
soda water, to top up

Put the ice cubes in an old-fashioned glass. Dash the grenadine over the ice, then pour in the pernod and vodka. Top up with soda water.

Vodka Salty Dog
Serves I
fine sea salt
6–8 ice cubes
I measure vodka
4 measures grapefruit juice

Dampen the rim of a large goblet with a little water or grapefruit juice then dip the rim into a saucer of fine sea salt. Fill the prepared glass with ice. Add the vodka and grapefruit juice and stir.

White Spider
Serves I
2 measures vodka
I measure clear crème de menthe
crushed ice (optional)

Pour the vodka and crème de menthe into a cocktail shaker. Shake and pour into a chilled cocktail glass or over crushed ice.

Xantippe

Haven

White Russian

Serves I

6 cracked ice cubes
I measure vodka
I measure Tía María
I measure milk or double cream

Put half the ice cubes in a cocktail shaker and add the vodka, Tía María and milk or double cream. Shake until a frost forms. Put the remaining ice cubes in a tall narrow glass and strain the cocktail over them. Serve with a straw.

Black Russian

Serves I

4–6 cracked ice cubes
2 measures vodka
I measure Kahlúa
chocolate stick, to decorate (optional)

Put the cracked ice in a short glass. Add the vodka and Kahlúa and stir. Decorate with a chocolate stick, if you like.

Moscow Mule

Serves I

3–4 cracked ice cubes
2 measures vodka
juice of 2 limes
ginger beer, to top up
lime or orange slices, to decorate

Put the cracked ice in a cocktail shaker. Add the vodka and lime juice and shake until a frost forms. Pour into a tall glass, top up with ginger beer and stir gently. Decorate with lime or orange slices.

Bullshot

Serves I

6 ice cubes (optional)
I½ measures vodka
4 measures beef consommé (hot or chilled)
I dash Worcestershire sauce
salt and pepper

Put the ice cubes, if using, in a cocktail shaker and add the vodka, consommé and Worcestershire sauce and season lightly with salt and pepper. Shake well. Strain into a large glass or a handled glass, if serving hot.

Variation

This is said to be a good hangover cure. As a variation, try I measure vodka, I measure tomato juice and I measure beef consommé. Mix the ingredients in a tall glass half-filled with ice. Add a squeeze of lemon.

Vodka Grasshopper

Serves I

I½ measures vodka
I½ measures green crème de menthe
I½ measures crème de cacao
crushed ice

Pour the vodka, crème de menthe and crème de cacao into a cocktail shaker half-filled with ice. Shake and strain into a chilled cocktail glass.

Black Russian (left) and White Russian

Moscow Mule

Using up stocks

The Moscow Mule is one of those happy accidents. It was invented in 1941 by an employee of a US drinks firm in conjunction with a Los Angeles bar owner who was overstocked with ginger beer.

Party Pieces

This sparkling collection of lively cocktails will make any party a sure-fire success, from the tried-and-tested Vodka Martini to the more modern Millennium Cocktail. In fact, just serving them will turn any occasion into a special celebration.

Vodka Sour

Serves 1

4–5 ice cubes
2 measures vodka
½ measure sugar syrup (see page 4)
1 egg white
1½ measures fresh lemon juice
3 drops Angostura bitters, to decorate

Put the ice cubes in a cocktail shaker, add the vodka, sugar syrup, egg white and lemon juice and shake until a frost forms. Pour without straining into a cocktail glass and shake 3 drops of Angostura bitters on the top to decorate.

Vodka Martini

Serves 1

4–5 cracked ice cubes
¼ measure dry vermouth
3 measures vodka
green olive or lemon rind spiral, to decorate

Put the ice cubes in a mixing glass. Pour the vermouth and vodka over the ice and stir vigorously. Strain into a chilled cocktail glass, drop in the green olive or decorate with a spiral of lemon rind.

Blue Champagne

Serves 1

4–6 ice cubes
1 measure vodka
2 tablespoons fresh lemon juice
2–3 dashes Curaçao
2–3 dashes blue Curaçao
chilled Champagne, to top up

Put the ice cubes in a cocktail shaker, add the vodka, lemon juice, Curaçao and blue Curaçao and shake well. Strain into a Champagne flute and top up with Champagne.

Variation

Another vodka and Champagne combination is the Bucked-up Fizz. Pour 2 measures orange juice and ½ measure vodka into a Champagne flute. Top up with Champagne.

Head-over-Heels

Serves 1

4–5 ice cubes
juice of 1 lime or lemon
1 teaspoon sugar syrup (see page 4)
3 measures vodka
3 drops Angostura bitters
Champagne, to top up
strawberry, to decorate

Put the ice cubes in a cocktail shaker. Pour the lime or lemon juice, sugar syrup, vodka and bitters over the ice and shake until a frost forms. Pour without straining into a highball glass, top up with Champagne and decorate with a strawberry.

Vodka Sour

Vodka Martini

Did you know?
In some circles the Vodka Martini is known as a Kangaroo.

Millennium Cocktail

Serves 1

4–5 cracked ice cubes
1 measure vodka
1 measure fresh raspberry juice
1 measure fresh orange juice
4 measures Champagne or sparkling dry white wine, chilled

Put the ice cubes in a cocktail shaker, add the vodka, raspberry juice and orange juice and shake until a frost forms. Strain into a Champagne glass and pour in the Champagne.

Bellini-tini

Serves 1

4–5 cracked ice cubes
2 measures vodka
½ measure peach schnapps
1 teaspoon peach juice
Champagne, to top up
peach slices, to decorate

Put the ice cubes in a cocktail shaker and add the vodka, peach schnapps and peach juice. Shake until a frost forms. Strain into a chilled cocktail glass and top up with Champagne. Decorate with peach slices.

Road Runner

Serves 1

6 cracked ice cubes
2 measures vodka
1 measure Amaretto di Saronno
1 measure coconut milk (see page 17)
grated nutmeg, to decorate

Put the cracked ice in a cocktail shaker and add the vodka, Amaretto and coconut milk. Shake until a frost forms, then strain into a cocktail glass. Sprinkle with a pinch of grated nutmeg.

One of Those

Serves 1

4–6 ice cubes
1 measure vodka
4 measures cranberry juice
2 dashes Amaretto di Saronno
juice of ½ lime
lime slice, to decorate

Half-fill a highball glass with ice cubes. Pour the vodka, cranberry juice, Amaretto and lime juice into a cocktail shaker. Shake thoroughly, pour into the highball glass and decorate with a lime slice.

Snapdragon

Serves 1

4–6 ice cubes
2 measures vodka
4 measures green crème de menthe
soda water, to top up
mint sprig, to decorate

Fill a highball glass with ice cubes. Add the vodka and crème de menthe and stir. Top up with soda water. Decorate with a mint sprig.

Millennium Cocktail

Bellini-tini

Cosmopolitan

Serves 1

6 cracked ice cubes
1 measure vodka
½ measure Cointreau
1 measure cranberry juice
juice of ½ lime
lime slice, to decorate

Put the cracked ice in a cocktail shaker and add the vodka, Cointreau, cranberry juice and lime juice. Shake until a frost forms. Strain into a cocktail glass and decorate with a lime slice.

Madras

Serves 1

6–8 ice cubes
1 measure vodka
1 measure orange juice
2 measures cranberry juice
orange or lime slice, to decorate

Half-fill a tall glass with ice. Pour over the vodka, orange juice and cranberry juice and decorate with a fruit slice.

Machete

Serves 1

4–6 ice cubes
1 measure vodka
2 measures pineapple juice
3 measures tonic water

Fill a tall glass or wine glass with ice cubes. Pour the vodka, pineapple juice and tonic into a mixing glass. Stir, then pour into the glass of ice.

Vodka Twister Fizz

Serves 1

4–5 ice cubes
juice of 1 lemon
½ teaspoon sugar syrup (see page 4)
1 egg white
3 drops pernod
3 measures vodka
ginger ale, to top up
lime slice, to decorate

Put the ice cubes in a cocktail shaker. Pour the lemon juice, sugar syrup, egg white, pernod and vodka over the ice and shake until a frost forms. Pour without straining into a highball glass and top up with ginger ale. Stir once or twice and decorate with a lime slice.

Down-under Fizz

Serves 1

4–5 ice cubes
juice of 1 lemon
juice of ½ orange
½ teaspoon grenadine
3 measures vodka
soda water, to top up

Put the ice cubes in a cocktail shaker. Pour the lemon juice, orange juice, grenadine and vodka over the ice and shake until a frost forms. Pour without straining into a highball glass and top up with soda water. Serve with a straw.

Cosmopolitan

Vodka Twister Fizz

Downunder Fizz

Vodka, Lime and Soda

Serves 1

6–8 ice cubes
1 measure vodka
2 measures lime cordial or lime juice
soda water, to top up
lime slice, to decorate

Vodka Sea Breeze

Serves 1

5 ice cubes, crushed
1 measure vodka
1½ measures cranberry juice
1½ measures fresh grapefruit juice
lime slice, to decorate

Put the crushed ice in a tall glass, pour over the vodka, cranberry juice and fresh grapefruit juice and stir well. Decorate with a lime slice and serve with a straw.

Variation

To make a Cape Cod(der), mix 1 measure vodka, 2 measures cranberry juice and add 1 dash lemon juice.

Half-fill a tall glass with ice cubes. Pour in the vodka and lime cordial or lime juice, top up with soda water and stir. Decorate with a lime slice.

Polish Honey Drink

Serves 8

6 tablespoons clear honey
300 ml (½ pint) water
4 cloves
7.5 cm (3 inch) piece of cinnamon stick
1 vanilla pod
2 long lemon rind strips
2 long orange rind strips
1 bottle vodka (750 ml/1¼ pints)

Put the honey and water in a saucepan and heat gently until the honey has dissolved. Add the cloves, cinnamon stick, vanilla pod, lemon rind and orange rind. Bring to the boil and simmer for 5 minutes. Cover the pan, remove from the heat and leave to infuse for 1 hour. Strain and return to the rinsed pan. Add the vodka and bring to just below simmering point over a low heat and warm through for 5 minutes. Serve in warmed, handled glasses or mugs.

Vodka Limeade

Serves 8

6 limes
125 g (4 oz) caster sugar
750 ml (1¼ pints) boiling water
salt
8 measures vodka
ice cubes
lime wedges, to decorate

Halve the limes, then squeeze the juice into a large jug. Put the squeezed halves in a heatproof bowl with the sugar and boiling water and leave to infuse for 15 minutes. Add a pinch of salt, give the infusion a good stir then strain it into the jug with the lime juice and add the vodka. Add 6 ice cubes, cover and refrigerate for 2 hours, or until chilled. To serve, place 3–4 ice cubes in each glass and pour the limeade over them. Decorate each glass with a lime wedge.

Warsaw Cocktail

Serves 1

6 ice cubes
1 measure vodka
½ measure blackberry-flavoured brandy
½ measure dry vermouth
1 teaspoon fresh lemon juice

Put the ice cubes in a cocktail shaker and add the vodka, brandy, dry vermouth and lemon juice. Shake until a frost forms. Strain into a cocktail glass and serve.

Vodka Sea Breeze

Vodka Limeade

Exotic and Fruity

The versatility of vodka is amply demonstrated here. Mix it with fruit, fruit juice, liqueurs, cream, ice cream or spices to set the taste buds tingling. Whether you choose Frozen Steppes, Siamese Slammer or Caribbean Cruise, you will be transported with delight.

Siamese Slammer

Serves 4

3 measures vodka
juice of 2 oranges
1 small ripe papaya, peeled and chopped
1 banana, sliced
juice of 1 lime
3 measures sugar syrup (see page 4)
8 ice cubes, crushed
4 papaya slices, to decorate

Put all the ingredients in a blender and process until smooth. Serve in tall glasses, each decorated with a slice of papaya.

Cool Wind

Serves 1

4–5 ice cubes
1 measure dry vermouth
juice of ½ grapefruit
½ teaspoon Cointreau
3 measures Vodka

Put the ice cubes in a mixing glass. Pour the vermouth, grapefruit juice, Cointreau and vodka over the ice. Stir gently, then strain into a chilled cocktail glass.

Chi Chi

Serves 1

2 measures vodka
1 measure coconut cream (see page 17)
4 measures pineapple juice
6 ice cubes, crushed
to decorate
pineapple slice
cocktail cherry

Put the vodka, coconut cream, pineapple juice and crushed ice in a blender and process until smooth. Pour into a tall glass and decorate with a slice of pineapple and a cherry.

Blue Moon

Serves 1

5 cracked ice cubes
¾ measure vodka
¾ measure tequila
1 measure blue Curaçao
lemonade, to top up

Put half the ice in a mixing glass and add the vodka, tequila and blue Curaçao. Stir to mix. Put the remaining ice in a tall glass; strain in the cocktail. Top up with lemonade and serve with a straw.

Cranberry Crush

Serves 10

600 ml (1 pint) cranberry juice
600 ml (1 pint) fresh orange juice
150 ml (¼ pint) water
½ teaspoon ground ginger
½ teaspoon mixed spice
sugar, to taste
1 bottle vodka (750 ml/1¼ pints)
to decorate
kumquats
cranberries
mint sprigs

Place the cranberry juice, orange juice, water, ground ginger and mixed spice in a saucepan and bring to the boil over a low heat. Stir in sugar to taste, then simmer for 5 minutes. Remove from the heat and stir in the vodka. Pour into punch cups and decorate with kumquats, cranberries and mint sprigs. Alternatively, serve chilled for a summer party.

Siamese Slammer

Cranberry Crush

Vodka and Watermelon Crush

Serves 2–3

I large or 2 small ripe watermelons, chilled
300 ml (½ pint) fresh orange juice
juice of I lime
3 measures vodka
sugar, to taste
crushed ice
watermelon slices, to decorate

Cut the watermelon into quarters and remove the skin and seeds. Roughly chop the flesh and put it in a food processor or blender with the orange juice, lime juice and vodka. Add sugar to taste and process until smooth. Fill 2–3 glasses with crushed ice and pour in the drink. Add a watermelon slice to each glass to decorate.

Sloe Comfortable Screw

Serves I

6–8 ice cubes
½ measure sloe gin
½ measure Southern Comfort
I measure vodka
2½ measures orange juice

Half-fill a tall glass with ice cubes. Pour the sloe gin, Southern Comfort, vodka and orange juice into the glass and stir well.

Variation
To make a Sloe Comfortable Screw up Against the Wall, mix the drink as above and top with Galliano.

Did you know?
The final part of the cocktail's name derives from the place where the tall, slender bottle of Galliano is usually kept in a bar.

Frozen Steppes

Serves I

I measure vodka
I measure dark crème de cacao
I scoop vanilla ice cream
cocktail cherry, to decorate

Put the vodka, crème de cacao and ice cream in a blender and process for a few seconds. Pour into a large wine glass and decorate with a cocktail cherry.

Creamsickle

Serves I

6 cracked ice cubes
I measure vodka
I measure Curaçao
I measure white crème de cacao
I measure single cream

Put the cracked ice in a cocktail shaker and add the vodka, Curaçao, crème de cacao and single cream. Shake until a frost forms, then pour into a highball glass.

Vodka Daiquiri

Serves I

6 cracked ice cubes
I measure vodka
I teaspoon sugar
juice of ½ lime or lemon

Put the cracked ice in a cocktail shaker and add the vodka, sugar and lime or lemon juice. Shake until a frost forms. Strain into a cocktail glass.

*Vodka and
Watermelon Crush*

Frozen Daiquiris

To make a frozen vodka daiquiri, combine
the vodka, sugar and lime or lemon juice
in a blender with a handful of crushed
ice. Process for a few seconds on low
speed, then at high speed until firm.
Decorate with a slice of lime and a
cherry and serve with a straw.

Cherry Vodka Julep

Serves 1

8 cracked ice cubes
juice of ½ lemon
1 teaspoon sugar or sugar syrup (see page 4)
1 teaspoon grenadine
1 measure cherry brandy
3 measures vodka
1 measure sloe gin
to decorate
lemon slice
orange slice

Fill a tall glass with cracked ice. Put 3–4 ice cubes in a mixing glass and pour in the lemon juice, sugar or sugar syrup, grenadine, cherry brandy, vodka and sloe gin. Stir, then strain the drink into the ice-filled glass. Decorate with the lemon and orange slices.

Melon Ball

Serves 1

5 cracked ice cubes
1 measure vodka
1 measure Midori (see page 13)
1 measure orange juice, plus extra to top up
to decorate
orange slice
small banana ball

Put the cracked ice in a tall glass or goblet. Pour the vodka, Midori and orange juice into a cocktail shaker. Shake well to mix, then strain into the glass. Top up with more orange juice if necessary. Decorate with the fruit and serve with a straw.

Caribbean Cruise

Serves 1

10–12 ice cubes
1 measure vodka
¼ measure light rum
¼ measure coconut rum
1 dash grenadine
2 measures pineapple juice
pineapple slice, to decorate

Put 6 ice cubes in a cocktail shaker and add the vodka, both kinds of rum and the grenadine. Shake until a frost forms. Half-fill a tall glass with ice cubes, strain the cocktail over the ice and add the pineapple juice. Decorate with a pineapple slice.

Sex on the Beach

Serves 1

3 ice cubes
½ measure vodka
½ measure peach schnapps
1 measure cranberry juice
1 measure orange juice
1 measure pineapple juice (optional)
cocktail cherry, to decorate

Put the ice in a cocktail shaker and add the vodka, peach schnapps, cranberry juice, orange juice and pineapple juice, if using. Shake until a frost forms. Pour into a tall glass, decorate with the cherry and serve with a straw.

Melon Ball

Vodka Caipirinha
Serves I
6 lime wedges
2 teaspoons brown sugar
2 measures vodka
crushed ice

Place 3 of the lime wedges in a large tumbler or old-fashioned glass and add the brown sugar and vodka. Mix well, mashing the lime wedges slightly to release a little juice. Top up with crushed ice and decorate with the remaining lime wedges.

Mudslide
Serves I
10 cracked ice cubes
I measure vodka
I measure Kahlúa
I measure Baileys Irish Cream

Put 6 cracked ice cubes in a cocktail shaker and add the vodka, Kahlúa and Baileys. Shake until a frost forms. Strain into a tumbler and add the remaining cracked ice.

Russian Coffee
Serves I
½ measure vodka
½ measure coffee liqueur
½ measure double cream
crushed ice

Put the vodka, coffee liqueur, cream and crushed ice in a blender and process for about 15 seconds. Strain into a cocktail glass and serve.

Tip
Before taking a sip of this drink, why not toast to your health with the customary Russian and Polish toast *na zdrowie?*

Hawaiian Vodka
Serves I
4–5 ice cubes
I measure pineapple juice
juice of I lemon
juice of I orange
I teaspoon grenadine
3 measures vodka
lemon slice, to decorate

Put the ice cubes in a cocktail shaker. Add the pineapple juice, lemon juice, orange juice, grenadine and vodka and shake until a frost forms. Strain into a tumbler, decorate with a lemon slice and serve with a straw.

Vodka Caipirinha

awaiian Vodka

Did you know?

The Caipirinha is a vodka variation of the authentic cocktail, which is traditionally made with cachaça, a Brazilian spirit distilled from rum and sugar cane.

Baileys Irish Cream is a cream liqueur made of Irish whiskey, chocolate and double cream.

Monkey's Delight

Serves 1

1 measure vodka
½ measure crème de bananes
½ measure dark crème de cacao
1 banana
2 scoops vanilla ice cream
½ measure single cream

Put the vodka, crème de bananes, crème de cacao, three-quarters of the banana, the ice cream and cream in a blender and process until smooth. Pour into a tall glass. Decorate with the reserved banana, cut into slices.

Hairy Fuzzy Navel

Serves 1

6 cracked ice cubes
1 measure peach schnapps
1½ measures vodka
1 tablespoon orange juice

Put the cracked ice in a cocktail shaker and add the peach schnapps, vodka and orange juice. Shake until a frost forms, then strain into a cocktail glass.

Variation

A Fuzzy Navel is made without the vodka.

Lemon Drop

Serves 1

6 cracked ice cubes
1 measure vodka
lemon wedge
sugar, for dipping

Put the cracked ice in a cocktail shaker, add the vodka and shake until a frost forms. Strain into a shot glass. Dip the lemon wedge in the sugar. Drink the vodka, then suck on the lemon immediately.

Kamikaze

Serves 1

6 cracked ice cubes
½ measure vodka
½ measure Curaçao
½ measure lime juice

Put the cracked ice in a cocktail shaker and add the vodka, Curaçao and lime juice. Shake until a frost forms, then strain into a shot glass.

Kamikaze

Tequila Cocktails

Tequila

Tequila has an exotic quality that is missing from the other major spirits. Distilled from the root of the maguey or blue agave, a cactus-like plant which looks like a huge pineapple, tequila is Mexico's contribution to the great drinks of the world. With its strong flavour, tequila has now become a standard ingredient in the well-stocked cocktail bar.

Jalisco's Unique Spirit

Pulque was the first drink to be produced from the agave. It is made by fermenting the sap from the plant, and dates back to prehispanic times. A low-alcohol drink, it is still drunk today. When the Spaniards conquered Mexico in 1519–21, one of the many things they introduced was the art of distilling and they experimented with pulque. During the late eighteenth and early nineteenth century it was realized that the best *aguardiente de agave*, as the distilled spirit was known, was produced around the town of Tequila in the state of Jalisco in southern Mexico. By the late nineteenth century the commercial cultivation of agaves in Mexico had begun and by the 1870s there were about a dozen distilleries. The United States was the first, and is still the most important, export market for tequila, but it was not until the mid-1960s that tequila burst upon the rest of the world. By the 1970s the demand had led to a need for regulations to define tequila and protect the name, limiting its production to tequila produced in the state of Jalisco.

Tequila and Mezcal

Tequila has been described as having a smooth sharpness. There are several types. Tequila blanco, the original, is colourless, while tequila reposado (gold) is aged in oak barrels for up to 11 months. Tequila añejo has longer ageing. Mezcal is an another agave-distilled spirit but with a different style. Mezcals labelled *'con gusano'* contain a worm. Despite widespread belief, tequila does not contain a worm.

How to Drink Tequila

The traditional way to drink tequila is with a pinch of salt. The practice is to lick the salt from between the thumb and forefinger, then knock back the tequila from a shot glass and suck a wedge of lime or lemon. Salt is also used for rimming the glass of the Margarita, a concoction of tequila, Cointreau and fresh lime juice. It originated in the late 1930s at the hotel bar in the Rancho la Gloria, Rosarita Beach, Tijuana, where it was thought to be created by Danny Herrera for the actress Marjorie King, who was allergic to all spirits except tequila. He named it Margarita – the Spanish for Marjorie.

Agave Julep (see page 112)

Margaritas

Dating from the late 1930s, the Margarita is the most famous of all tequila cocktails and, because it is such a great drink, it has inspired a host of variations.

Original Margarita

Serves 1
3 lime wedges
fine sea salt
1¼ measures tequila
¾ measure Cointreau
1¼ measures fresh lime juice
4–5 ice cubes
lime slice, to decorate

Dampen the rim of a chilled cocktail glass with one of the lime wedges then dip the rim into fine sea salt. Pour the tequila, Cointreau and lime juice into a cocktail shaker. Squeeze the juice from the remaining two lime wedges into the shaker, squeeze the wedges to release the oils in the skin then drop the wedges into the shaker. Add the ice cubes and shake vigorously for about 10 seconds. Strain the cocktail into the chilled glass and decorate with a lime slice.

Cadillac

Serves 1
3 lime wedges
fine sea salt
1¼ measures tequila gold
½ measure Cointreau
1¼ measures fresh lime juice
4–5 ice cubes
2 teaspoons Grand Marnier
lime slice, to decorate

Dampen the rim of a chilled cocktail glass with one of the lime wedges, then dip the rim into fine sea salt. Pour the tequila, Cointreau and lime juice into a cocktail shaker. Squeeze the juice from the two remaining lime wedges into the shaker, pressing the rind to release its oils. Drop the wedges into the shaker. Add the ice cubes and shake vigorously for 10 seconds then strain the drink into the glass. Drizzle the Grand Marnier over the top and decorate with a lime slice.

Floreciente

Serves 1
orange slice
fine sea salt
crushed ice
1¼ measures tequila gold
¾ measure Cointreau
¾ measure fresh lemon juice
¾ measure fresh blood orange juice
blood orange wedge, to decorate

Dampen the rim of an old-fashioned glass with an orange slice then dip the glass into fine sea salt and fill it with crushed ice. Pour the tequila, Cointreau, lemon juice and blood orange juice into a cocktail shaker, shake vigorously for 10 seconds then strain into the old-fashioned glass. Decorate with a blood orange wedge.

Cadillac

Original Margarita

Pink Cadillac Convertible

Serves 1

3 lime wedges
fine sea salt
ice cubes
1¼ measures tequila gold
½ measure Cointreau
¾ measure fresh lime juice
¾ measure cranberry juice
¾ measure Grand Marnier
lime wedge, to decorate

Dampen the rim of an old-fashioned glass with one of the lime wedges, then dip the rim into fine sea salt and fill the glass with ice cubes. Pour the tequila, Cointreau, lime juice and cranberry juice into a cocktail shaker. Squeeze the juice from the two remaining lime wedges into the shaker, pressing the rind to release its oils. Drop the wedges into the shaker. Add 4–5 ice cubes and shake vigorously for 10 seconds then strain the drink into the glass. Decorate with a lime wedge. Pour the Grand Marnier into a shot glass and serve it on the side. The Grand Marnier should be poured on top of the cocktail just before drinking.

Cobalt Margarita

Serves 1

lime wedge
fine sea salt
1¼ measures tequila
2 teaspoons Cointreau
½ measure blue Curaçao
¾ measure fresh lime juice
¾ measure fresh grapefruit juice
4–5 ice cubes
lime rind spiral, to decorate

Dampen the rim of a chilled cocktail glass with a lime wedge then dip it into fine sea salt. Pour the tequila, Cointreau, blue Curaçao, lime juice and grapefruit juice into a cocktail shaker. Add the ice cubes and shake vigorously for 10 seconds then strain into the cocktail glass. Decorate with a lime rind spiral.

Tip

To make a citrus spiral, pare the rind from the fruit with a canelle knife or vegetable peeler then wind it tightly around a glass swizzle stick.

Playa del Mar

Serves 1

orange slice
light brown sugar and sea salt mixture
ice cubes
1¼ measures tequila gold
¾ measure Grand Marnier
2 teaspoons fresh lime juice
¾ measure cranberry juice
¾ measure fresh pineapple juice
to decorate
pineapple wedge
orange rind spiral

Dampen the rim of a sling glass with the orange slice then dip the glass into the brown sugar and sea salt mixture. Fill the glass with ice cubes. Pour the tequila, Grand Marnier, lime juice, cranberry juice and pineapple juice into a cocktail shaker. Fill the shaker with ice cubes and shake vigorously for 10 seconds then strain into the sling glass. Decorate the glass with a pineapple wedge and an orange rind spiral.

Pink Cadillac Convertible

balt Margarita

Playa del Mar

Ruby Rita
Serves I
1¼ measures fresh pink grapefruit juice
fine sea salt
ice cubes
1¼ measures tequila gold
¾ measure Cointreau
pink grapefruit wedge, to decorate

Dampen the rim of an old-fashioned glass with some pink grapefruit juice and dip it into fine sea salt. Fill the glass with ice cubes. Pour the tequila, Cointreau and pink grapefruit juice into a cocktail shaker, fill it with more ice and shake vigorously. Strain into the old-fashioned glass and decorate with a pink grapefruit wedge.

Forest Fruit
Serves I
lime wedge
brown sugar
2 blackberries
2 raspberries
2 teaspoons Chambord (see opposite)
2 teaspoons crème de mure (see opposite)
1¼ measures tequila
2 teaspoons Cointreau
1¼ measures fresh lemon juice
crushed ice
to decorate
lemon slices
blackberry
raspberry

Dampen the rim of an old-fashioned glass with a lime wedge and dip it into brown sugar. Drop the blackberries and raspberries into the glass and muddle to a pulp with the back of a spoon. Stir in the Chambord and crème de mure. Pour in the tequila, Cointreau and lemon juice, fill with crushed ice and stir gently, lifting the muddled berries from the bottom of the glass. Decorate with lemon slices, a blackberry and a raspberry.

Maracuja
Serves I
I fresh ripe passion fruit
1¼ measures tequila gold
I tablespoon Creole Shrub (see opposite)
¾ measure fresh lime juice
2 teaspoons Cointreau
I teaspoon passion fruit syrup
4–5 ice cubes
physalis (Cape gooseberry), to decorate

Cut the passion fruit in half and scoop the flesh into a cocktail shaker. Add the tequila, Creole Shrub, lime juice, Cointreau, passion fruit syrup and ice cubes and shake vigorously for 10 seconds. Strain through a small fine sieve into a chilled cocktail glass. Decorate with a physalis.

by Rita

Did you know?

Chambord is a black raspberry liqueur and crème de mure is a blackberry one.

Creole Shrub is a golden-coloured rum, flavoured with orange peel.

Forest Fruit

Maracuja

Cool Classics

These delectable mixes show you just what glorious cocktails can be based on tequila and mezcal – from Tequini (the local equivalent of a Martini) and Mezcarita to Bloody Maria and Coco Loco.

South of the Border

Serves I

1¼ measures tequila
¾ measure Kahlúa
1¼ measures fresh lime juice
4–5 ice cubes

Pour the tequila, Kahlúa and lime juice into a cocktail shaker. Add the ice cubes and shake vigorously for 10 seconds then strain into a chilled cocktail glass.

Did you know?

Kahlúa is as Mexican as tequila. It is a liqueur made from Mexican coffee beans.

Tequini

Serves I

ice cubes
3 dashes orange bitters
75 ml (3 fl oz) tequila blanco
2 teaspoons dry French vermouth, preferably Noilly Prat
black olive, to decorate

Fill a mixing glass with ice cubes then add the orange bitters and tequila. Stir gently with a bar spoon for 10 seconds. Take a chilled cocktail glass and add the vermouth, film the inside of the glass with the vermouth then tip it out. Stir the bitters and tequila for a further 10 seconds and strain into the chilled glass. Decorate with a black olive.

Alleluia

Serves I

¾ measure tequila
½ measure blue Curaçao
2 teaspoons maraschino syrup
I dash egg white
¾ measure fresh lemon juice
ice cubes
100 ml (3½ fl oz) bitter lemon
to decorate
lemon slice
cocktail cherry
mint sprig

Pour the tequila, blue Curaçao, maraschino syrup, egg white and lemon juice into a cocktail shaker, add 4–5 ice cubes and shake vigorously. Fill a highball glass with ice cubes and strain the drink over the ice. Top up with the bitter lemon and stir gently. Decorate with a lemon slice, cherry and mint sprig.

Tip

For maraschino syrup, use the syrup from the jar of cocktail cherries.

Mezcarita

Serves I

lemon wedge
chilli salt
1¼ measures mezcal
¾ measure Cointreau
1¼ measures fresh lemon juice
4–5 ice cubes
lemon rind spiral, to decorate

Dampen the rim of a chilled cocktail glass with the wedge of lemon and dip it into chilli salt. Pour the mezcal, Cointreau and lemon juice into a cocktail shaker, add the ice cubes and shake vigorously. Strain into the cocktail glass and decorate with the lemon rind spiral.

outh of the Border

Tequini

Mexican martini

The Tequini is the Mexican equivalent of a martini, with tequila replacing the gin and the orange bitters adding an exotic tang. It is one of the few drinks decorated with a black olive rather than a green one.

Sour Apple

Serves I

1¼ measures tequila
2 teaspoons Cointreau
1 tablespoon apple schnapps
¾ measure fresh lime juice
¾ measure dry apple juice
4–5 ice cubes
Granny Smith apple wedge, to decorate

Pour the tequila, Cointreau, apple schnapps, lime juice and apple juice into a cocktail shaker, add the ice cubes and shake vigorously for 10 seconds then strain into a chilled cocktail glass. Decorate with the apple wedge.

Chapala

Serves I

1¼ measures tequila
¾ measure Cointreau
¾ measure fresh lemon juice
¾ measure fresh orange juice
2 teaspoons grenadine
orange rind spiral, to decorate

Pour the tequila, Cointreau, lemon juice and orange juice into a cocktail shaker. Add the grenadine and shake vigorously for 10 seconds then strain into a chilled cocktail glass. Decorate with an orange rind spiral.

Ananas and Coco

Serves I

1¼ measures tequila gold
¾ measure coconut syrup
1 large chunk fresh pineapple
1¼ measures pineapple juice
crushed ice
pineapple wedge, to decorate

Put the tequila, coconut syrup, pineapple chunk and juice in a blender. Add a handful of crushed ice, blend for 20 seconds then pour into a wine goblet. Decorate with a pineapple wedge.

Honey Water

Serves I

4–5 ice cubes
1¼ measures tequila gold
¾ measure sweet vermouth
3 dashes Angostura bitters
3 dashes Peychaud bitters
2 teaspoons Grand Marnier
to decorate
cocktail cherry
orange rind spiral

Put the ice cubes in a mixing glass, pour in the tequila, vermouth and both bitters and stir gently for 10 seconds. Put the Grand Marnier in a chilled cocktail glass, film the inside of the glass with the Grand Marnier then tip it out. Stir the contents of the mixing glass again for 10 seconds then strain into the cocktail glass. Decorate with a cocktail cherry and an orange rind spiral.

Sour Apple

Honey Water

Bloody Maria
Serves 1

lime wedge
celery salt
black pepper
ice cubes
1¼ measures tequila
2 teaspoons medium sherry
2 dashes Tabasco sauce
4 dashes Worcestershire sauce
1 tablespoon fresh lime juice
100 ml (3½ fl oz) fresh tomato juice
cayenne pepper
4–5 ice cubes
to decorate
celery stick
lime wedge
basil sprig

Dampen the rim of an old-fashioned glass with a lime wedge then dip it into celery salt and black pepper. Fill a cocktail shaker with ice cubes then add the tequila, medium sherry, Tabasco sauce, Worcestershire sauce, lime juice, tomato juice and a pinch each of celery salt, black pepper and cayenne pepper. Add the ice cubes and shake vigorously then pour into the prepared glass. Decorate with the celery stick, lime wedge and a sprig of basil.

Mockingbird
Serves 1

1¼ measures tequila
¾ measure green crème de menthe
1¼ measures fresh lime juice
4–5 ice cubes
lemon rind spiral, to decorate

Pour the tequila, green crème de menthe and lime juice into a cocktail shaker. Add the ice cubes, shake vigorously for about 10 seconds then strain into a chilled cocktail glass. Decorate with a lemon rind spiral.

Frozen Strawberry
Serves 1

sugar
small handful of crushed ice
2 measures tequila
1 measure strawberry liqueur
1 measure fresh lime juice
4 ripe strawberries
1 teaspoon sugar syrup (see page 4)
fresh strawberry, unhulled, to decorate

Dampen the rim of a chilled cocktail glass and dip it into the sugar. Put the crushed ice in a blender and pour in the tequila, strawberry liqueur and fresh lime juice. Drop in the strawberries, add the sugar syrup and blend for a few seconds. Pour without straining into a cocktail glass and decorate with a strawberry.

Japanese Slipper
Serves 1

lime wedge
brown sugar
1¼ measures tequila
¾ measure Midori (see page 13)
1¼ measures fresh lime juice
4–5 ice cubes
lime wedge, to decorate

Dampen the rim of a chilled cocktail glass with a lime wedge then dip the rim into brown sugar. Pour the tequila, Midori and lime juice into a cocktail shaker and add the ice cubes. Shake vigorously for about 10 seconds then strain into the cocktail glass and decorate with a lime wedge.

Bloody Maria

Mockingbird

Pancho Villa

Serves 1

1 measure tequila
½ measure Tía María
1 teaspoon Cointreau
4–5 ice cubes
brandied cherry, to decorate (optional)

Pour the tequila, Tía María and Cointreau into a cocktail shaker. Add the ice cubes, shake vigorously for about 10 seconds, then strain into a cocktail glass. Decorate with a brandied cherry, if liked.

Tequila Sunset

Serves 1

1 measure tequila gold
1 measure fresh lemon juice
1 measure fresh orange juice
1 tablespoon honey
crushed ice
lemon rind spiral, to decorate

Put the tequila in a chilled cocktail glass, add the lemon juice and then the orange juice and stir. Drizzle the honey into the glass so that it falls in a layer to the bottom, add the crushed ice and decorate with a lemon rind spiral.

Coco Loco

Serves 1

¾ measure white rum
¾ measure tequila
½ measure vodka
1 measure coconut cream (see page 17)
2 measures fresh lemon juice
3 cracked ice cubes
to decorate
lemon rind spiral
cocktail cherries

Pour the rum, tequila, vodka, coconut cream and lemon juice into a blender. Mix for 15 seconds. Put the ice cubes in a large goblet and pour the cocktail over them. Decorate with the lemon rind spiral and cherries and drink with a straw.

Pancho Villa

Tequila Sunset

Coco Loco

Long Shots

In this collection of cocktail recipes, fruit juices of all sorts and fruit liqueurs blend deliciously with tequila and ice to make a series of long refreshing drinks.

Texas Tea

Serves 1
¾ measure tequila
1 tablespoon white rum
1 tablespoon Cointreau
2 teaspoons sugar syrup (see page 4)
¾ measure fresh lemon juice
¾ measure fresh orange juice
100 ml (3½ fl oz) strong fruit tea, chilled
ice cubes
to decorate
orange slice
lemon slice
mint sprig

Pour the tequila, rum, Cointreau, sugar syrup, lemon juice, orange juice and tea into a cocktail shaker, add a handful of ice cubes and shake vigorously. Fill a sling glass with fresh ice cubes and strain the drink over them. Decorate with orange and lemon slices and a mint sprig.

Tip
One of the best teas to use as a base for this refreshing drink is a mixed berry tea. Its essential fruitiness blends very well with the citrus juices in Texas Tea.

Mexicola

Serves 1
4 lime wedges
crushed ice
1¼ measures tequila
150 ml (¼ pint) Coca Cola

Put the lime wedges in a highball glass and crush gently with a pestle to release the juices and oils. Fill the glass with crushed ice, then pour in the tequila and Coca Cola. Stir gently, lifting the lime wedges through the drink.

Matador

Serves 1
1¼ measures tequila
¾ measure fresh lime juice
100 ml (3½ fl oz) pineapple juice
1 pineapple chunk
2 teaspoons sugar syrup (see page 4)
crushed ice
to decorate
pineapple wedge
lime rind spiral

Put the tequila, lime juice, pineapple juice, pineapple chunk and sugar syrup in a blender. Add a handful of crushed ice and blend for 15 seconds. Pour into a highball glass and decorate with a pineapple wedge and a lime rind spiral.

Tijuana Sling

Serves 1
1¼ measures tequila
¾ measure crème de cassis
¾ measure fresh lime juice
2 dashes Peychaud bitters
4–5 ice cubes
100 ml (3½ fl oz) ginger ale
to decorate
lime slice
fresh blackcurrants or blueberries

Pour the tequila, crème de cassis, lime juice and Peychaud bitters into a cocktail shaker. Add the ice cubes and shake vigorously. Pour into a sling glass then top up with the ginger ale. Decorate with a lime slice and fresh berries.

Texas Tea

Tijuana Sling

Agave Julep

Serves 1

8 torn mint leaves
1 tablespoon sugar syrup (see page 4)
1¼ measures tequila gold
1¼ measures fresh lime juice
crushed ice
to decorate
lime wedge
mint sprig

Put the mint leaves in a highball glass and cover with the sugar syrup. Muddle with a pestle to release the mint oils. Add the tequila and lime juice, fill the glass with crushed ice and stir vigorously. Decorate with a lime wedge and a mint sprig.

El Diablo

Serves 1

ice cubes
1½ measures tequila gold
¾ measure fresh lime juice
2 teaspoons grenadine
100 ml (3½ fl oz) ginger ale
lime slice, to decorate

Fill a highball glass with ice cubes, then pour in the tequila gold, fresh lime juice and grenadine. Top up with the ginger ale and stir gently. Decorate with a lime slice.

Sunburn

Serves 1

ice cubes
¾ measure tequila gold
1 tablespoon Cointreau
150 ml (¼ pint) cranberry juice
orange slice, to decorate

Fill a highball glass with ice cubes, then pour in the tequila, Cointreau and cranberry juice. Decorate with an orange slice.

Rosarita Bay Breeze

Serves 1

ice cubes
1¼ measures tequila
150 ml (¼ pint) cranberry juice
1¼ measures pineapple juice
orange slice, to decorate

Put the ice cubes in a highball glass and pour in the tequila and cranberry juice. Float the pineapple juice over the top of the drink and decorate with an orange slice.

Agave Julep

Fruity ice
cubes

Decorative ice cubes make an unusual finishing touch for drinks. Half-fill an ice cube tray with water and freeze until firm. Prepare pieces of citrus rind or mint sprigs and dip into cold water. Add to the ice tray and freeze again. Top up with water and freeze until firm.

Tequila Sunrise

Serves 1
5–6 ice cubes
1 measure tequila
100 ml (3½ fl oz) fresh orange juice
2 teaspoons grenadine
to decorate
star fruit slice
orange slice

Crack half the ice cubes and put them in a cocktail shaker. Add the tequila and orange juice and shake to mix. Put the remaining ice in a tall glass and strain the tequila into it. Slowly pour in the grenadine and allow it to settle. Just before serving, stir once. Decorate the glass with the star fruit and orange slice.

Gold Digger

Serves 1
ice cubes
¾ measure tequila gold
¾ measure golden rum
150 ml (¼ pint) fresh orange juice
2 teaspoons Grand Marnier
orange slice, to decorate

Put some ice cubes in a highball glass. Pour in the tequila, rum and orange juice and stir gently. Drizzle over the Grand Marnier and decorate with an orange slice.

Rooster Booster

Serves 1
ice cubes
1¼ measures tequila
150 ml (¼ pint) fresh grapefruit juice
1 tablespoon grenadine
100 ml (3½ fl oz) soda water
to decorate
lime slice
cocktail cherry

Put some ice cubes in a highball glass. Pour in the tequila, grapefruit juice and grenadine, stir gently then top up with the soda water. Decorate with a lime slice and a cherry.

Mexicana

Serves 1
8–10 ice cubes
1¼ measures tequila
¾ measure Framboise
¾ measure fresh lemon juice
100 ml (3½ fl oz) pineapple juice
to decorate
pineapple wedge
lemon slice

Put 4–5 ice cubes in a highball glass. Pour the tequila, Framboise, lemon juice and pineapple juice into a cocktail shaker. Add 4–5 ice cubes and shake vigorously for about 10 seconds. Strain into the highball glass and decorate with a pineapple wedge and a lemon slice.

Did you know?
Framboise is an *alcool blanc*, a fruit liqueur (in this case a raspberry one) which is stored in glass rather than wood and so does not acquire any colour from the cask while it matures.

Tequila Sunrise

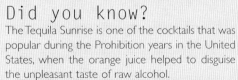

Did you know?
The Tequila Sunrise is one of the cocktails that was popular during the Prohibition years in the United States, when the orange juice helped to disguise the unpleasant taste of raw alcohol.

Thai Sunrise

Serves 1
½ ripe mango, peeled and sliced
¾ measure tequila
1 tablespoon Cointreau
1 teaspoon grenadine
¾ measure fresh lime or lemon juice
¾ measure sugar syrup (see page 4)
2–3 cracked ice cubes
lime slices, to decorate

Put all the ingredients in a food processor and blend until the ice is crushed. Pour into an old-fashioned glass and decorate with lime slices.

Baja Sour

Serves 1
1¼ measures tequila gold
2 teaspoons sugar syrup (see page 4)
1¼ measures fresh lemon juice
2 dashes orange bitters
½ egg white
4–5 ice cubes
1 tablespoon amontillado sherry
to decorate
lemon slices
orange rind spiral

Pour the tequila, sugar syrup, lemon juice, orange bitters and egg white into a cocktail shaker. Add 4–5 ice cubes and shake vigorously. Pour into a sour glass and drizzle over the sherry. Decorate with lemon slices and an orange rind spiral.

Pepper Eater

Serves 1
ice cubes
1¼ measures tequila
¾ measure Cointreau
100 ml (3½ fl oz) cranberry juice
1¼ measures fresh orange juice
orange slice, to decorate

Fill a tall glass with ice cubes. Pour in the tequila, Cointreau, cranberry juice and orange juice and stir gently. Decorate with an orange slice.
Tip
Rolling an orange or any other citrus fruit hard on a board before you squeeze it helps extract more juice.

Brooklyn Bomber

Serves 1
5 ice cubes, crushed
1 measure tequila
½ measure Cointreau
½ measure cherry brandy
½ measure Galliano
1 measure lemon juice
to decorate
orange slice
cocktail cherry

Put half the ice in a cocktail shaker and add the tequila, Cointreau, cherry brandy, Galliano and lemon juice. Shake to mix. Put the remaining ice in a hurricane glass and pour in the drink. Decorate with the orange slice and cherry and serve with straws.

Thai Sunrise

Brooklyn Bomber

Tequila de Coco

Serves I

small handful of crushed ice
I measure tequila
I measure fresh lemon juice
I measure coconut syrup
3 dashes maraschino (black cherry liqueur)
lemon slice, to decorate

Put the crushed ice in a blender and add the tequila, fresh lemon juice, coconut syrup and maraschino. Blend for a few seconds then pour the drink into a Collins glass and decorate with a lemon slice.

Jalisco Swizzle

Serves I

crushed ice
3 dashes Angostura bitters
¾ measure tequila gold
¾ measure golden rum
1¼ measures fresh lime juice
¾ measure passion fruit juice
2 teaspoons sugar syrup (see page 4)
4–5 ice cubes
¾ measure soda water
to decorate
lime slice
mint sprig

Fill a chilled highball glass with crushed ice. Shake the bitters into a cocktail shaker, pour in the tequila, rum, lime juice, passion fruit juice and sugar syrup. Add the ice cubes and shake vigorously then strain into the highball glass. Top up with soda water and stir briefly until the glass frosts. Decorate with a lime slice and a mint sprig.

Acapulco

Serves I

cracked ice
I measure tequila
I measure white rum
2 measures pineapple juice
I measure fresh grapefruit juice
I measure coconut syrup
ice cubes
pineapple wedge, to decorate

Put some cracked ice in a cocktail shaker and pour in the tequila, rum, pineapple juice, grapefruit juice and coconut syrup. Fill a tall glass with ice cubes. Shake the drink and pour it over the ice. Decorate with a pineapple wedge and serve with straws.

Desert Daisy

Serves I

crushed ice
I measure tequila
1¼ measures fresh lime juice
2 teaspoons sugar syrup (see page 4)
I tablespoon crème de fraises des bois
to decorate
blackberry
strawberry
lime wedge
orange wedge
mint sprig

Half-fill an old-fashioned glass with crushed ice. Pour in the tequila, lime juice and sugar syrup and stir gently until the glass frosts. Add more crushed ice then float the crème de fraises des bois on top. Decorate with a blackberry, a strawberry, a lime wedge, orange wedge and a mint sprig.

Acapulco

Cream of the Cactus

The exotic flavours and generous servings of fresh cream in this collection of recipes add a rich smoothness to tequila cocktails. You need to be on your guard with these drinks as the cream disguises the strength of the alcohol.

Silk Stocking
Serves I
drinking chocolate powder
¾ measure tequila
¾ measure white crème de cacao
100 ml (3½ fl oz) single cream
2 teaspoons grenadine
4–5 ice cubes

Dampen the rim of a chilled cocktail glass and dip it into the drinking chocolate powder. Pour the tequila, white crème de cacao, cream and grenadine into a cocktail shaker and add the ice cubes. Shake vigorously for 10 seconds then strain into the chilled cocktail glass.

Brave Bull
Serves I
ice cubes
¾ measure tequila
¾ measure Kahlúa

Fill an old-fashioned glass with ice cubes, pour in the tequila and Kahlúa and stir gently.
Variation
To turn a Brave Bull into a Brown Cow, add 1¼ measures single cream and stir to blend it in. To turn a Brave Bull into a Raging Bull, add 1 teaspoon flaming Sambuca.

Sombrero
Serves I
¾ measure tequila gold
¾ measure white crème de cacao
100 ml (3½ fl oz) single cream
4–5 ice cubes
grated nutmeg, to decorate

Pour the tequila, crème de cacao and cream into a cocktail shaker. Add the ice cubes and shake vigorously for 10 seconds then strain into a chilled cocktail glass. To decorate, sprinkle the top of the drink with grated nutmeg.
Did you know?
Crème de cacao, the chocolate liqueur, comes in two versions, dark and white. Choose according to how you want your drink to look. Combining the dark version in a Sombrero with tequila gold and cream would result in a subtle coffee-coloured drink.

Silk Stocking

Sombrero

Mexican Bulldog

Serves 1
ice cubes
¾ measure tequila
¾ measure Kahlúa
1¼ measures single cream
100 ml (3½ fl oz) Coca Cola
drinking chocolate powder, to decorate

Put some ice cubes in a highball glass. Pour in the tequila, Kahlúa and cream then top up with the Coca Cola. Stir gently and serve decorated with drinking chocolate powder.

Acapulco Bliss

Serves 1
¾ measure tequila
1 tablespoon Pisang Ambon (banana liqueur)
2 teaspoons Galliano
¾ measure fresh lemon juice
¾ measure single cream
100 ml (3½ fl oz) passion fruit juice
4–5 ice cubes
to decorate
lemon slices
pineapple wedge
mint sprig

Pour the tequila, Pisang Ambon, Galliano, lemon juice, cream and passion fruit juice into a cocktail shaker; add the ice cubes and shake vigorously. Pour into a sling glass and decorate with lemon slices, a pineapple wedge and a mint sprig. Drink with straws.

Frostbite

Serves 1
4–5 ice cubes
1 measure tequila
1 measure double cream
1 measure white crème de cacao
½ measure white crème de menthe
drinking chocolate powder, to decorate

Put the ice cubes in a cocktail shaker. Pour in the tequila, cream, crème de cacao, and crème de menthe and shake vigorously for 10 seconds. Strain into a chilled cocktail glass and sprinkle with drinking chocolate powder.

Mexican Bulldog

Did you know?
Pisang Ambon is a Dutch, fruit-based liqueur made mainly from bananas and made to an old Indonesian recipe.

Acapulco Bliss

Frostbite

Index of Cocktails

Mai Tai	18	Pink Rum	26	Sunset Tea	32
Maiden's Prayer	42	Pink Treasure	28	Sydney Fizz	52
Maracuja	100	Planter's Punch	26	**T**equila de Coco	118
Margarita	96	Playa del Mar	98	Tequila Sunrise	114
Martini	38	Poet's Dream	56	Tequila Sunset	108
Matador	110	Polish Honey Drunk	80	Tequini	102
Melon Ball	86	Port Antonio	18	Texas Tea	110
Melon Daiquiri	12	Punch Julien	28	Thai Sunrise	116
Mexican Bulldog	122	Pussyfoot	22	Tijuana Sling	110
Mexicana	114	**R**aging Bull	120	Tobago Fizz	26
Mexicola	110	Red Kiss	58	Tropical Dream	22
Mezcarita	102	Road Runner	76	**V**irgin's Prayer	22
Millennium Cocktail	76	Rooster Booster	114	Vodka and Watermelon	
Mississippi Punch	24	Rosarita Bay Breeze	112	Crush	84
Mockingbird	106	Ruby Rita	100	Vodka Caipirinha	88
Monkey Gland	42	Rum Martini	30	Vodka Collins	68
Monkey's Delight	90	Russian Coffee	88	Vodka Daiquiri	84
Moon River	56	**S**t Lucia	20	Vodka Gibson	68
Morning Glory Fizz	52	Salty Dog	54	Vodka Grasshopper	72
Moscow Mule	72	Sapphire Martini	48	Vodka Limeade	80
Mudslide	88	Screwdriver	66	Vodka, Lime and Soda	80
New Orleans Dandy	26	Sea Breeze	52	Vodka Martini	74
New Orleans Dry		Serenade	20	Vodka Salty Dog	70
Martini	38	Sex on the Beach	86	Vodka Sazerac	68
Night of Passion	46	Siamese Slammer	82	Vodka Sea Breeze	80
One of Those	76	Silk Stocking	120	Vodka Sour	74
Opera	38	Singapore Gin Sling	52	Vodka Twister Fizz	78
Orange Blossom	42	Sloe Comfortable Screw	84	**W**arsaw Cocktail	80
Pancho Villa	108	Slow Comfortable Screw		White Lady	40
Paradise	42	Up Against The Wall	84	White Russian	72
Peach Blow	48	Snapdragon	76	White Spider	70
Pepper Eater	116	Sombrero	120	White Witch	32
Pina Colada	16	Sour Apple	104	Woodstock	60
Pink Cadillac		South of the Border	102	**X**antippe	70
Convertible	98	Stormy Weather	60	**Y**ellow Gin	54
Pink Clover Club	40	Strawberry Daiquiri	12	**Z**ombie	14
Pink Gin	54	Summertime	18	Zombie Christophe	14
Pink Lady	40	Sunburn	112	Zombie Prince	14

Index of Ingredients

Bold numbers refer to 'Did you know?' boxes

Acknowledgements

Executive Editor **Nicola Hill**
Editor **Abi Rowsell**
Senior Designer **Joanna Bennett**
Designer **Ginny Zeal**
Production Controller **Louise Hall**

Picture Credits:
© Octopus Publishing Group Ltd.
Jean Cazals: 75 (bottom). / Sandra Lane: 65 ; 91 (top).
David Loftus: front cover (top left); spine (bottom); 7 (bottom right). / Neil Mersh: 5 (top left); 7 (top), (bottom left); 11 (top and bottom); 13 (top); 15 (top right), (bottom);17 (top); 19 (top right); 21 (top); 23 (bottom); 25 (bottom right); 27 (top left), (bottom left), (bottom right); 31 (bottom left); 34 (bottom left); 37; 39 (top left), (top right); 41 (top), (bottom right); 43 (top left); 49 (bottom right); 51 (top and bottom); 53 (top left), (bottom); 55 (top), (bottom left); 59 (top and bottom); 69 (top left), (top right); 75 (top right); 77 (top and bottom); 79 (bottom); 85 (bottom); 87 (left); 89 (top and bottom); 97 (top right).
Peter Myers: front cover (bottom right); 19 (bottom right); 25 (bottom left); 43 (bottom); 45 (bottom right); 63 (bottom); 83 (bottom left).
Peter Myers/ Neil Mersh: 109 (bottom right); 117 (top right).
William Reavell: back cover (top and bottom); front cover (top rght) (bottom left); 5 (top right), (bottom); 8 (top and bottom); 13 (bottom); 15 (top left); 17 (bottom); 19 (top left); 21 (bottom); 22 (bottom); 23 (top); 25 (top left); 29 (top); 31 (top), (bottom right); 33 (top), (bottom left), (bottom right); 35 (top), (bottom right); 40 (bottom left); 43 (top right); 45 (top), (bottom left); 47 (top), (bottom); 49 (bottom left); 55 (bottom right); 57 (bottom left), (bottom right); 61 (bottom right); 63 (top), (bottom right); 67 (top), (bottom left); 69 (bottom); 71 (top), (bottom left), (bottom right); 73 (top); 75 (top left); 77 (bottom right); 81 (top), (bottom left), (bottom right); 83 (top left), (top right), (bottom right); 85 (top left), (top right); 87 (top right), (bottom right); 91 (bottom); 93 (top left), (top right), (bottom left), (bottom right); 95 (left and right); 97 (top left), (bottom left), (bottom right); 99 (top), (bottom left), (bottom right); 100 (top), (bottom left), (bottom right); 103 (top left), (top right), (bottom right); 105 (top left), (top right), (bottom); 107 (top), (bottom left), (bottom right); 109 (top), (bottom left); 111 (top left), (top right), (bottom right); 113 (top), (bottom left), (bottom right); 115 (top), (bottom); 117 (top left), (bottom); 119 (top), (bottom); 121 (top), (bottom left), (bottom right); 123 (top), (bottom left), (bottom right).